John Cooney *has pro*_____ *onal and*
clinically *sub*_____ *of alcohol*
abuse. His *bo*___ *richly* _____ *clinician*
and teacher _____ *self as the*
most experien___ *spec*___ _____ *clinical accounts*
provide a re*markable and detailed* _____ *physical,*
psychological and social consequence of the misuse of alcohol. *A very prac-*
tical and forthright book.

Professor A.W. Clare

A wealth of knowledge and unrivalled experience in *the treatment of alcohol-*
ism combine with compassionate good sense to make this very readable
book most valuable for every person touched by the problem of alcoholism.

Neil M. — AA member

Of the many books written in recent years about alcoholics and problem
drinkers this one is outstanding in that it is primarily based from
the author's innumerable hours of discussions with and observations of
alcoholics over many years. Everyone affected by and interested in problem
drinking can learn a great deal from studying John Cooney's excellent
volume.

Dr M.M. Glatt

The author shares the wisdom and insights of a lifetime dedicated to the
treatment of alcoholism in humane, straightforward language which will
inform the general public and greatly enhance the work of physicians,
nurses, counsellors, clergy and teachers. This is a timely book which
eloquently addresses the many issues of universal concern about alcohol
problems.

Professor Tom McGovern

To all those victims of alcohol abuse
and their families
from whom
I have learned so much down through the years

UNDER THE WEATHER

Alcohol Abuse and Alcoholism

HOW TO COPE

John G. Cooney

GILL AND MACMILLAN

Published in Ireland by
Gill and Macmillan Ltd
Goldenbridge
Dublin 8
with associated companies in
Auckland, Delhi, Gaborone, Hamburg, Harare,
Hong Kong, Johannesburg, Kuala Lumpur, Lagos, London,
Manzini, Melbourne, Mexico City, Nairobi,
New York, Singapore, Tokyo
© John G. Cooney, 1991
Reprinted 1991
0 7171 1861 4
Index compiled by Helen Litton
Print origination by
Seton Music Graphics, Bantry, Co. Cork
Printed by
Colour Books Ltd, Dublin

Contents

Introduction

THIS BOOK is based on a series of lectures which I prepared and delivered at St Patrick's Hospital, Dublin over a number of years. They were constructed to incorporate the basic facts concerning alcohol abuse and alcoholism, as well as pointing the way to recovery, and were constantly updated in the light of new information.

The lectures are an amalgam of material derived from many sources over a long period of time, i.e. articles, journals, pamphlets, textbooks, seminars, conferences and most particularly, countless interviews with victims of alcohol abuse and their families. They formed the basis for the Alcohol Programme conducted at St Patrick's Hospital.

St Patrick's Psychiatric Hospital was founded in 1745 by the celebrated author and philanthropist Jonathan Swift, Dean of St Patrick's Cathedral. His philanthropy in respect of St Patrick's Hospital has been immortalised in his own verse.

> He gave the little wealth he had
> To build a house for fools and mad:
> And showed by one satiric touch
> No nation wanted it so much.

The hospital is a voluntary, non-denominational, non-profit-making institution under the control of a Board of Governors who serve on a voluntary basis. It still operates on its original site adjacent to the historic part of Dublin known as the Liberties. Over the years it has been refurbished and remodelled with many new buildings added, notably the Dean Swift wing in 1985, in order to provide the facilities necessary for modern psychiatric practice. Each year it caters for a large number of patients drawn from all parts of Ireland, and, in some cases, from abroad. These men and women are treated on both an in-patient and out-patient basis as is deemed appropriate.

For many years St Patrick's has been engaged in the treatment of persons suffering from alcohol dependence and alcohol abuse. Indeed the hospital could be said to be one of the pioneers of the formal treatment of alcoholism in the western world. In recent years it has not only concentrated on developing its treatment programme through the establishment of a specialist multidisciplinary team, but has also been active in the areas of prevention and education, while engaging in research into different aspects of alcohol abuse and alcoholism. On projects of common interest, the hospital works closely with Trinity College, Dublin whose medical students receive their training in psychiatry at St Patrick's, as well as with other agencies, both statutory and voluntary, in the field of psychiatry in Ireland and abroad.

For reasons of convenience and conciseness only, the masculine pronoun has been used throughout.

Acknowledgments

MY THANKS and gratitude are due to a number of people.

In the first instance to Rolande Anderson, Assistant Director of the Alcohol Programme at St Patrick's Hospital, the Honourable Mr Justice Declan Costello, SC, Conor F. and Professor Brendan Kennelly for their contributions which have greatly enhanced this book.

In particular, I am indebted yet again to Rolande Anderson for his chapter on 'The Family'.

I am pleased to have the opportunity to express my gratitude to all staff at St Patrick's Hospital for their co-operation and assistance over the years. In a special way, I am most grateful to the members of the Alcohol Team whose expertise and dedication have been instrumental in bringing so many of our alcoholic patients to recovery, as well as providing solace for their families. I consider that I have been both privileged and fortunate to have worked so closely with each one of them.

I shall always be grateful to Professor J. N. P. Moore for stimulating my interest in alcohol abuse and alcoholism and providing the opportunity for me to work in this field. I am very conscious of how much I owe to his successor, Professor P. J. Meehan, for his constant encouragement and wise counsel. Professor Anthony Clare has been most helpful in the preparation and production of this book. My gratitude is due also to the Board of Governors of St Patrick's Hospital for their ready support for my work.

Many people have helped with practical suggestions and comments, notably Dr Harry Barniville, Mrs Joan Carr, Dr Denis Conniffe (ESRI), Dr Max Glatt, Neil M. of AA, Professor Thomas McGovern, Dr Matt Murphy, and Mrs Mary O'Hagan.

In writing this book I have received much appreciated assistance from my secretary, Mrs Olive Lally, and from the Secretary/Manager of St Patrick's Hospital, Noel Breslin.

The preparation of the material was carried out with her customary skill and efficiency by Miss Pat Moloney.

I welcome the opportunity to acknowledge the expert advice so courteously and efficiently provided by Michael Gill and his colleagues in Gill and Macmillan.

This book would not have been possible without the never-failing support of my wife, Patricia, and that of my family. I am eternally grateful to them for their tolerance of the encroachment on our family life resulting from the many demands on my time brought about by a busy professional career.

Healer

(For Dr John Cooney)

The horror of accusing morning light
Condemns me to another hideous day.
Did someone cry? What did I do last night?
Was someone hurt? Insulted? What did I say?
My hands are crazy, blood streaks my eyes,
Jeering images flash havoc through my mind,
My mouth is full of muck and stupid lies,
I'm hell, I know hell's taste and smell and sound.

Healer, I hear you speak: your head and heart
Help many a suffering man and woman
While I, like countless women and men,
Am learning how to tend and heal each hurt
With candid, gentle words, profoundly human.
Thanks to you, hope lives again.

BRENDAN KENNELLY

Foreword

THERE WILL be few who pick up this book who will not have witnessed, perhaps in their own families, perhaps amongst their colleagues or friends, the pain and suffering which alcoholism causes and will not have seen at least one life devastated by it. For alcoholism is a widespread and pervasive disorder, no respecter of persons, and is to be found in every walk of life and every class of society; but it is also one which is widely misunderstood, not least by those who suffer from it. Not surprisingly it is a subject which has produced a large literature, engendered much debate (and not a little conflict) and those who suffer from it and those who may wish to help the sufferers may well be at a loss to know where to turn to learn of its causes, or how best to handle the many problems associated with it.

I was, then, glad to learn that Dr Cooney had agreed to publish this book which is the distillation of reflections on a lifetime's experience of helping those and their families who suffer from alcohol abuse as well as conclusions reached from a deep knowledge of the subject.

St Patrick's Hospital in Dublin has played an active, indeed unique, role in this country in the treatment of alcoholism, in research on the subject and in the promotion of educational courses to combat it. Dr Cooney, Director of its Alcoholic Programme, has for many years been intimately involved in this work, but his involvement has not been confined to clinical experience. To help stimulate public awareness, public action and research on the problem, he helped to found the Irish National Council on Alcoholism and for many years served in a voluntary capacity on its Board, Executive Committee and as Chairman of its Research Committee. He has written widely on the subject, lectured on it in this country, the United Kingdom and the United States of America, and represented Ireland at many international conferences.

For many years Dr Cooney gave a series of popular lectures on various aspects of alcoholism. They were notable for the clarity of their expression and the balance of their approach. He has brought the same qualities to this work (which would please the Great Dean who founded St Patrick's!) and it will deservedly attract a wide readership anxious for information and assistance in this important area.

DECLAN COSTELLO
Judge of the High Court

Formerly Chairman of the
Irish National Council on Alcoholism

1

Alcoholism — a Disease

The Disease Concept

IN PRACTICAL terms, alcoholism or alcohol dependency is best regarded as a disease in the modern meaning of that term, i.e. as a bio-psycho social condition. This is the view of such prestigious bodies as the American National Council on Alcoholism and the Royal College of Psychiatrists in London. For a full definition see Appendix A.

An argument often advanced against this notion of the disease concept is that if it is too vigorously pursued, in effect one is giving the alcoholic a licence to drink again: 'Doctor, I could not help taking that first drink because I suffer from the disease of alcoholism.' This is not a valid objection. Any properly conducted programme for the treatment of alcoholism will emphasise the fact that the primary responsibility for recovery rests with the alcoholic himself.

When an alcoholic comes for treatment he should be furnished with what is in effect a written contract, in which it is clearly set out that (a) it is recognised and accepted that nobody *consciously* sets out to develop alcoholism, but (b) once the condition is established — and this fact is spelled out to the individual concerned — then he must take the primary responsibility for his own recovery. It is made clear that every possible help will be afforded to the alcoholic and his family to achieve this objective. At the same time, it is stressed that their chances of success are high, provided they are prepared to apply themselves wholeheartedly to the treatment programme.

Over the years, I have never met one alcoholic among the many thousands with whom I have been in contact who has consciously set out to develop the condition. This is a basic fact which is so often overlooked.

If one takes a representative sample of ten persons suffering from alcoholism, one would expect to find 7–8 men and 2–3 women in such a group. There will be in this sample old people, young people, clever people, stupid people, rich people, poor people, some from rural areas, some from the city or town, people of considerable importance in their own community as well as those with a relatively low profile. And yet, if one takes an individual history from each of these ten people making up the group, it is soon apparent that every one of them, in effect, is telling the same story, allowing for some individual variations. In other words, here is a disparate group of people with different backgrounds, levels of intelligence, affluence, etc. volunteering similar signs and symptoms and displaying a common pattern of behaviour brought about by their drinking habits.

Moreover, I have found that when I attend conferences on alcohol abuse in the UK, in Europe or in the USA, within a few minutes I can identify readily with the different speakers who are all dealing with the same problems present every working day in Ireland.

For the moment, let us consider the proposition that alcoholism is not a disease but merely a bad habit, self-inflicted. It follows that one is no longer dealing with victims of a disease but rather with persons of poor character or moral weakness. This means that we have thus reverted to the 'sin' model of alcoholism prevalent up to the 1930s when AA (Alcoholics Anonymous) came into being. Now the alcoholic can no longer expect to receive the understanding to which he is entitled.

I well remember, many years ago, talking to a recovered alcoholic who helped us greatly with our work. He rarely spoke of his own drinking days, but one evening he surprised me by stating rather bitterly, in a fashion which was quite out of character for him, that in his 'bad days' he did not look for sympathy from anyone but did expect understanding, particularly from the doctors whom he consulted and who failed him for so long in this respect.

I fear that if this disease concept of alcoholism is rejected, the enlightenment and understanding of the condition, which have been so painfully and laboriously gained over the years, will be lost, and the public support for the proper and compassionate treatment of alcoholism seriously eroded.

The Alcoholic

Those who suffer from alcoholism are called alcoholics. This is a term which is often misunderstood and gives rise to much difficulty. The longer I work in the field of alcohol abuse the more reluctant I am to use the word 'alcoholic', until I am certain that those with whom I am attempting to communicate define the term as I do myself. There is no mystery involved.

The working definition which I employ is that put forward years ago by Marty Mann in her book *Primer on Alcoholism* (Henry Holt and Co., 1950, New York). She defined an alcoholic as anyone whose drinking caused a continuing problem in any department of his or her life. This problem has to be continuing. There is no point, for instance, in the irate housewife castigating her husband as an alcoholic because he went out one night with 'the boys' and drank too much. Next day he missed work and scolded everyone in the home in a most unreasonable manner. This one fall from grace, so to speak, would not make the errant husband an alcoholic. Equally, the successful business or professional man or woman or housewife who is drinking abnormally, cannot claim that he or she is not an alcoholic merely because he or she still holds down a job or still has some degree of standing in his or her family or community life. When the position is examined, it is commonly found that the individual's affluence or financial standing is not nearly as sound as it should be, given his income, while the family relationships are almost inevitably undermined because of the drinking pattern.

Therefore, when we talk about an alcoholic we are not making any moral value judgment. We are merely stating that the individual concerned, man or woman, lay or cleric, young or old, rich or poor, clever or stupid, has reached a stage where alcohol is causing a continuing problem in some department of his or her life.

The Folklore of Alcoholism

The confusion in respect of the definition of the term 'alcoholic' reflects a wider and more deep-seated misunderstanding of the nature of alcoholism itself. This is bound up with what I term the 'folklore of alcoholism', made up of myths and fallacies which have gradually been accepted over the years. Their existence has interfered considerably with a proper appreciation of the true nature of alcoholism and they need to be vigorously debunked.

Each of us is conditioned to a lesser or greater extent by values and beliefs which we learn and accept early in life within our family circle. In turn, these have commonly been reinforced by our education and by our social circumstances. No matter how intelligent, discerning or perceptive we consider ourselves to be, each of us is the victim of this conditioning to a greater extent than we may appreciate.

Perhaps I might best deal with some of the myths and fallacies surrounding alcoholism by using rhetorical questions:

(a) *'Doctor, I could not be an alcoholic.'*
'Why not?'
'Because I don't drink very much. I associate consistently with five or six other lads, all of whom drink much more than I do. By any standard, none of them is an alcoholic and, therefore, since I drink less than they do, I could not be one.'

This is a myth. Remember that essentially it is not the amount of alcohol consumed which is the determining factor in diagnosis, but rather one's reaction to whatever amount one drinks. I have seen many 'true blue' alcoholics who have drunk relatively little alcohol, by comparison with the more common picture of the heavy-intake characteristic of the majority of alcoholics, and yet these people have been as truly victims of the disease as those who drank a great deal more. Hence, the importance of not making comparisons, but rather assessing everybody's drinking pattern on an individual basis.

4

(b) *'Doctor, I could not be an alcoholic.'*
   'Why not?'
   'Because I drink only beer and very rarely drink spirits.'

This too is a myth. All forms of intoxicating liquor sold legitimately contain a drug called ethyl alcohol. Essentially, alcoholism is addiction to ethyl alcohol which is not present in soft drinks. Apart from flavouring agents, the important difference between alcoholic drinks is the amount of ethyl alcohol present. For instance, beer contains 4% to 5% ethyl alcohol, table wine up to 13%, sherry approximately 15% to 16%, while spirits have in excess of 30%. It therefore follows that if one drinks a number of bottles of beer one is consuming as much ethyl alcohol as if one drank several glasses of Scotch or Irish whiskey.

(c) *'Doctor, I could not be an alcoholic.'*
   'Why not?'
   'Because I can go for periods of time without taking a drink. Last year, to placate the wife who was being very difficult about my drinking, I gave it up for six weeks!'

This means nothing in terms of diagnosis. Indeed, one might query why such a big fuss is made of giving up drinking. After all, the ordinary social drinker does not make an issue of it. One is reminded of Mark Twain's assertion that smoking was never a problem for him since he had given it up on hundreds of occasions!

It is important to remember that most alcoholics can exercise a certain degree of control over their consumption of alcohol for much of their drinking careers, even when they have progressed from social drinking to abnormal drinking. However, the more elderly the alcoholic, the more advanced he becomes in his alcoholism, or the poorer his physical health so often brought about by his abnormal drinking, the less likely is he to exercise even limited control. His drinking will now get out of control quite quickly and become obvious to those near to him.

(d) *'Doctor, I could not be an alcoholic.'*
   'Why not?'
   'Because I still hold down a job, I still maintain a reasonable social life and have support within my family circle.'

This is, of course, true of the great majority of alcoholics for most of their drinking careers. What you are saying in effect is that you could not be an alcoholic because you do not conform to the stereotype of the 'skid row' alcoholic, i.e. the individual who has lost family, friends and fortune to drink and has wound up on 'skid row'. Only a small proportion of alcoholics — 6% according to some authorities — reach this stage of degradation, so that the 'skid row' stereotype is very much the exception. Never forget that for many years the average alcoholic appears superficially no different from his peers.

Discussion

(a) *Quite often these days one hears the term 'problem drinker'. What does this mean?*
'Problem drinkers' are those whose lives may be affected to a lesser or greater extent by alcohol. In effect, the term embraces a spectrum ranging from intermittent and minor disabilities right through to full-blown alcoholism. Hence, the term should be applied with caution, as it is sometimes used by alcoholics to minimise, or even deny, the gravity of their drinking.

(b) *Is there any difference between the conditions of alcoholism and alcohol dependency?*
None.

(c) *How is an alcoholic diagnosed?*
First of all, questionnaires can be used which may give pointers (see Appendix B) to the possibility of the existence of alcoholism. Then there are various biochemical tests, none of which are necessarily conclusive in themselves but, if positive, can strongly support the diagnosis. This is especially true in respect of certain batteries of biochemical tests, i.e. when

the results of complementary specialised investigations are all positive. Basically, however, the diagnosis is made on clinical grounds. A careful drinking history is elicited against the background of the individual's total life history, with particular reference to such significant signs and symptoms as compulsion, impaired control, 'cures', withdrawal states and changes in tolerance for alcohol. Details of the family history should also be taken, with emphasis on the possible existence of psychiatric or drink problems. Ideally, an independent account along the same lines should always be sought from an individual or individuals with close knowledge of the patient under examination. This, of course, is conditional upon the patient's consent to such an enquiry.

In particular, the element of progression in respect of the drinking pattern and its effect on the life of the individual concerned, must be established.

(d) *What is the difference between somebody who abuses alcohol and an alcoholic?*
Individuals who experience a variety of social and medical problems as a result of high risk drinking but who are not dependent on alcohol, are termed alcohol abusers. Such people do not have the signs and symptoms listed in (c) above, and so are not classed as alcohol dependent or alcoholic. However it must be pointed out that the distinction can sometimes be difficult to establish. Moreover, alcohol abusers are at much more risk of developing alcohol dependence than are social drinkers.

(e) *Why is so much stress laid on the acceptance of alcoholism as a disease?*
I am convinced that were it not for the disease concept of alcoholism far fewer people would have come forward for help, and might not have been encouraged by their families and friends to do so. Here in Ireland this concept is being threatened at the present time. If we regress to the moralistic 'sin' model of long ago, then the victims of alcohol abuse will receive the second-class treatment deemed appropriate for victims of a bad habit, self-inflicted. This would mean that all the ground so laboriously gained over a number of

years in bringing about the present level of public enlightenment would be in danger of being lost and alcoholics and
their families forced to attempt to conceal the problem,
rather than confront it and seek the assistance so readily
available in the many treatment centres now functioning
throughout the country.

2

Alcoholism — Multifactorial Causation

OVER THE past ten to fifteen years our understanding of alcoholism has increased considerably. Even though a great deal more work needs to be done in this area, we are now much more certain as to why some drinkers become alcoholics.

We all have a tendency to advance simplistic solutions for complex problems. This approach is all too common in the field of alcohol abuse and alcoholism. One often hears the view, dogmatically expressed, that Mr Murphy became an alcoholic because he lost all his money; or conversely, it was by reason of his suddenly becoming affluent; or, to be facetious, that the same gentleman developed the problem because his mother-in-law died suddenly; or perhaps made an unexpected recovery from a serious illness, depending on his relationship with the lady in question!

We are now aware that no single factor brings about alcoholism. It is due to many causes and, hence, the multifactorial concept of the condition. Obviously, the relevance of the different factors varies from person to person. As an instance, the occupation of an individual (for example a worker in the drinks industry) might be highly significant for him but would be of little relevance to another victim of alcoholism. This illustrates the importance of taking into account the particular needs and characteristics of alcoholics, who must always be regarded and treated as individuals and not lumped together as a collection of cases of alcoholism. This principle needs to be borne in mind when one considers the schema which I will now outline in order to illustrate the multifactorial view of alcoholism. I would hope also that this outline will help towards an understanding of the nature of alcoholism itself.

A	Socio, Economic, Cultural			
B	Drug — Ethyl Alcohol			
C	Individual			
1	2	3	4	5
Biological Factors	Hereditary Factors	Psychological Factors	Psychosexual Factors	Mood Disorders

Socio, Economic, Cultural Factors

The first group of factors to be considered are best headed Socio, Economic, Cultural, and have received a great deal of attention in recent years. It is well established that those communities which have a tolerant attitude towards heavy drinking have a high incidence of alcoholism. France is a country which illustrates the point. By contrast, historically alcoholism is not as great a problem in Italy, a neighbouring Mediterranean country which has many cultural, social and religious characteristics in common with France. It is held that the reason for this difference is that heavy drinking, with all its consequences, is frowned upon in Italy, where it does not command the same level of tolerance that prevails in France. In turn, this difference in public attitude is based on economic reasons to a substantial extent. Many people earn their living in France in the production and retailing of wine and spirits. This situation has created a vested interest or lobby which condones the heavy drinking which has traditionally been such a feature of the French way of life.

Here in Ireland the position is not so clear cut. Our attitude to heavy drinking is described by the sociologists as 'ambivalent'. This is, of course, a very characteristic Irish attitude towards so many contentious matters. It is best summed up in such commonly employed terms as 'Well, I might and I mightn't', or, 'I would and I wouldn't'.

In this country we have a large number of people who favour heavy drinking. The fact that we now spend up to £4 m. per day on alcohol at a time of financial stringencies lends substance to the belief that many people in Ireland drink a great deal. Moreover, a recent calculation estimated that about 10% of our personal disposable income after income tax was spent on drink.

10

But impressive though these statistics may be, they do not give the full picture. In Ireland we have proportionately more young people under the age of 15 than any country in the European Community (EC), and their intake of alcohol is obviously not significant in terms of amount consumed. Moreover, our population has many elderly people whose consumption of alcohol is minimal. We all know that there are a substantial number of Pioneers or total abstainers in the country, as well as a very large number of persons who drink comparatively little. The national ambivalence towards alcohol is brought about by the contrasting attitudes of our heavy drinkers on the one hand, and those of our abstainers and moderate drinkers on the other.

Lest it be thought that all this theory is too general and not very relevant to any one individual, let me emphasise yet again, before coming to consider more specific factors, that all of us are influenced much more than we appreciate by the values and beliefs of the society to which we belong. We are first exposed to these in the family circle, and subsequently have them reinforced through education or participation in vocational and social life.

In practical terms this means that if one moves in a circle where there is a general acceptance and practice of heavy drinking, the odds are that one will follow the practice of the circle and indulge in heavy drinking oneself. For example, if one is a member of a sporting circle where the custom is to celebrate victory or drown one's sorrows in defeat with large quantities of alcohol, then one is likely to conform to this practice.

It is now accepted that if one follows a certain occupation one is more at risk. Those who indulge in expense-account entertaining, where clients are wined and dined for business reasons, come into this category. Similarly, people who work with drink, for example publicans, hoteliers and restaurateurs, are very much at risk of indulging in heavy drinking, as are politicians, journalists, public relations consultants, those in the entertainment world, as well as doctors. Do bear in mind also that if one is a member of certain cultural groups linked with the arts, one often finds oneself in an environment where heavy drinking is the order of the day. The myth of 'la vie Boheme' stretches back over the centuries. The notion that the taking of drink in large quantities in some way heightens creativity is a strongly rooted one. Many people still mistakenly believe that the artist will paint a masterpiece, the novelist produce a bestseller or the playwright an overnight success, with the aid of copious amounts of alcohol. Sadly, the opposite is the case. One has only to consider the careers of such people as F. Scott Fitzgerald, Dylan Thomas, Modigliani or Brendan Behan to appreciate that drink, in excess, kills creativity.

Ethyl Alcohol: A Drug

Now let us consider the second factor. All forms of intoxicating liquor sold legitimately contain ethyl alcohol. In essence, the difference between a soft drink and any type of intoxicating liquor is the presence of the drug ethyl alcohol in the intoxicating liquor. As outlined in Chapter 1, this is present to a lesser or greater degree in different drinks.

Ethyl alcohol is an addictive drug — a fact not generally accepted even by those drinkers who will vociferously denounce drug abuse. Even less commonly appreciated is the other basic fact that ethyl alcohol is a depressant. The first effect of alcohol is to relieve anxiety and dampen down inhibitions, hence the concept of alcohol as the 'domesticated drug'. This is why so many people, when exposed to stressful situations, turn to alcohol for relief and find themselves unwittingly using it as a drug.

Those who have experienced hangovers following excessive drinking will be only too well aware that their most distressing symptoms are feelings of 'doom and gloom'. These are due to the depressant effect of ethyl alcohol. It is essential that those who take a drink should be aware that alcohol is a depressant, and should never lose sight of this fundamental property of alcohol — even though its ability to relieve anxiety is much more apparent in the first instance.

The Individual Who Develops Alcoholism

The third group of factors is concerned with the individual who develops alcoholism. At this juncture, because our knowledge is not as precise as we would wish, the element of speculation comes more into the picture.

BIOLOGICAL FACTORS

The possibility often advanced of the existence of a biological factor is a good example of our predicament. For years past, many alcoholics have argued that they were born with some physical defect which meant that their bodies could not deal with or metabolise alcohol effectively. In essence, they suggested that they suffered from an inborn error of metabolism somewhat similar to PKU or Phenylketonuria. In this condition, the child is born without a substance necessary to break down protein foods. Should the PKU child be given these foods, he will suffer brain damage and become mentally handicapped. If, however, he is put on a special diet he will then go on to develop a normal level of intelligence.

From the viewpoint of the alcoholic, this is of course an attractive proposition. Not only does it remove all question of guilt, but it holds out the prospect that should such an inborn defect be discovered, then it might well be amenable to correction, and so the long awaited 'cure for alcoholism' would become a reality. The hard fact is that until recently there was very little solid evidence to sustain this theory. We are now aware, thanks to certain animal studies carried out in the USA, that there may be some truth in this theory after all. Further support is afforded from the studies of the brain tracings of children of alcoholics, which have been demonstrated to be significantly different from those taken, under similar conditions, of children of non-alcoholic parents.

HEREDITARY FACTORS

Tied in with this line of enquiry is a demonstration of the importance of heredity in alcoholism, a fact long suspected but now established beyond reasonable doubt, thanks mainly to studies in the USA and Scandinavia carried out on twins,

13

and on adoptees separated from their parents at an early age, as well as by animal experiments. One of the difficulties in carrying out these studies is to distinguish the effects of purely hereditary factors, such as those which determine the colour of one's eyes, height, weight, etc. from environmental causes. Any child growing up in an alcoholic family is inevitably exposed to considerable disharmony because of parental alcoholism. This leads to upset and a stunting of normal emotional development producing subsequent psychological problems. In turn, these children of alcoholic parents may well turn to alcohol in an attempt to relieve these problems. This is an example of alcoholism being determined as a result of the interaction between heredity and environment.

PSYCHOLOGICAL FACTORS

Psychological factors are obviously of considerable importance in causation. One theory put forward is that many alcoholics possess a 'low frustration threshold'. This means that they are less well fitted to stand up to the stresses and strains of everyday living, to which all of us are constantly exposed, than those with a better tolerance for frustration. In an attempt to obtain relief from the tension engendered by these stresses, they sometimes turn to alcohol, and in time find themselves increasingly relying on this socially accepted drug with resultant dependence. I believe there is much substance in this theory, from my own observation over the years of the striking rise in the frustration threshold of recovered alcoholics. These individuals have now become much more mature and better equipped to deal with the 'slings and arrows of outrageous fortune', which are all too often a part of the human condition.

We know also that those who are immature, unstable and inadequate in terms of their personality, are more at risk of developing alcohol problems because of the temptation to turn to alcohol in an attempt to relieve their difficulties. Let me emphasise that I am not stating that all alcoholics are immature, unstable and inadequate, but merely highlighting the vulnerability of those possessing these personality traits where alcohol is concerned. In the past, alcoholism was described as a personality disorder — quite wrongly, we now know, with the general acceptance of the modern multifactorial theory of causation.

PSYCHOSEXUAL FACTORS
Psychosexual problems are sometimes of significance: conditions such as impotence, frigidity, etc. Even in these days when there is much more openness on sexual matters, some people may be too shy or reticent to seek proper professional advice and guidance, and turn instead to alcohol to allay their anxiety and fears in this area.

MOOD SWINGS
And finally, we have to consider the significance of mood swings as determinants of alcohol abuse or alcoholism. I am referring here to pathological or abnormal mood swings which last longer and are much more intense than the normal 'ups and downs' which all of us experience from time to time and which, indeed, lend a variety to our lives which would otherwise be much more drab.

For many years, workers in the field of alcoholism have been conscious of a close connection between affective disorder (i.e. excessive mood swings) and alcoholism. In particular, people who become depressed are often unaware that they are suffering from an underlying disorder of body chemistry which produces a characteristic cluster of signs and symptoms. These include early morning wakening, where the individual cannot sustain his sleep but finds himself alert in the small hours of the morning with all kinds of morbid thoughts and fears running through his mind 'between midnight and dawn when the past is all deception and the future futureless'. Such individuals sometimes fall asleep just before it is time to rise and are then exhausted. Indeed, fatigue is a common symptom of depression. They experience a sense of futility and hate to face the day, believing that life has lost its savour. They sometimes tend to weep inappropriately. Their self-confidence is eroded, their concentration diminished, and their sex drive weakened. Quite often they lose their appetite for food with consequent loss of weight. Commonly they may become markedly irritable or, conversely, complain of being apathetic. Sometimes too,

15

they develop the conviction that their symptoms are due to an organic cause, for example heart disease or cancer. They now engage in a frustrating and fruitless search for a physical cause which will account for their condition. They may then confide their problem to some well-meaning but uninformed friend who will tell them confidently to 'pull themselves together' and take a drink to buck themselves up; and because alcohol is a depressant, they now run the grave risk of aggravating the depression and developing a drink problem in addition.

Elation is the other side of the coin to depression. Here, the subjects are 'too well'. They also tend to waken early, but instead of dwelling morbidly on their difficulties, real or imaginary, they are chafing to be up and about in order to put into operation their grandiose plans to bring off some major coup, reform society, or make a large fortune. They are over-active, over-talkative, with a pressure of speech and a flight of ideas in their minds. On occasions they tend to become sexually over-active. They become impatient and irritable and cannot accept that they are not well. They may indulge in drinking in a non-controlled fashion and will not accept that this is highly undesirable.

Some ten years ago, thanks to a generous grant from the Irish Distillers Company to the Irish National Council on Alcoholism, an elaborate research project was carried out on the connection between affective disorder and alcoholism on approximately 300 men who had been hospitalised for the treatment of alcoholism. It was found that in a large percentage of cases, affective disorders had been an important antecedent factor in determining their alcoholism. The results of this research have been published and widely accepted.

This then is the multifactorial theory of the etiology or the causation of alcoholism. Not every factor outlined will apply to each individual, nor will all the various factors themselves have the same relevance for every person afflicted with alcoholism.

Discussion

(a) *There is still a great deal to be learned about alcoholism. Is much research being done in this regard?*

All over the western world in particular, large sums of money and much effort are being expended to increase our knowledge. I believe that we are on the brink of many exciting new discoveries. In recent years the demonstration of the importance of heredity as a causative factor, and the ways in which it manifests itself, is most encouraging.

(b) *If a person is an alcoholic, does it mean that his children will automatically become alcoholics?*

No. Alcoholism is due to many factors of which heredity is only one, although highly important. Also, if an alcoholic has received adequate treatment it means that he has a knowledge of the disease, which will enable him to advise his children in respect of their drinking patterns in a manner that many other parents are not in a position to do. Obviously, children of alcoholic parents should be advised to be more prudent in respect of drink than their peers who come from non-alcoholic homes.

(c) *I know an alcoholic who had a high tolerance for alcohol early in his drinking career which enabled him to drink his friends 'under the table'. Did this help to make him an alcoholic?*

In our culture, the ability to hold one's liquor is held in such high esteem, that those young men in particular, who have developed this markedly increased tolerance are sometimes regarded as local heroes. Unfortunately, in effect this means that they are exposed to high doses of the addictive drug, ethyl alcohol, with a consequently greater risk of developing alcohol dependence.

(d) *Is an inferiority complex as important as some alcoholics claim it to be?*

I must declare my belief that I do not go along with the view that the inferiority complex is of major significance in alcoholism, if only for the reason that so many people who have not a problem with drink can identify readily with it.

17

(e) *How important are economic factors in the causation of alcoholism?*

Highly so. For instance spirits consumption is known to have increased by 250% from 1960 to 1987 — an increase which can be explained on the basis of income and price changes. Wine consumption has a very high income elasticity i.e. every 1% increase in income leads to a 1.6% increase in wine consumption which has quadrupled between 1960 and 1987. Relatively modest price changes will encourage switching from one drink to another. Highly significantly, however, very large across-the-board price rises would be required to reduce the consumption of all forms of alcoholic drinks.

(f) *If one follows a certain occupation, one is more at risk. Should a publican, for example, sell his licensed premises in order to stop drinking?*

This might not necessarily bring about the desired result. In fact, it might be counter-productive if he is unable to find a suitable alternative occupation. Obviously, the decision in respect of the sale of his bar is very much an individual one, to be carefully considered in the light of his particular circumstances. That said, it must be stressed however that the utilisation of his own inner resources in terms of motivation and a commitment to the implementation of the steps necessary for recovery, are more important than the sale of the bar, even though this might be considered desirable at the early stages of treatment.

(g) *Are we Irish particularly prone to alcohol problems?*

This is a view which is often expressed. Support for it is afforded by studies in the US on alcohol abuse in different immigrant groups, when the Irish were shown to be most affected by alcoholic problems. However, these findings do not necessarily prove the proposition.

3

Signs, Symptoms and Cross Addiction

Classical Signs of Alcoholism

Taken together, the classical signs and symptoms of alcoholism form a pattern indicative of how the condition manifests itself. Obviously, the disease will not present in exactly the same way in every case. This is yet another reason for treating victims of alcoholism as individuals rather than attempting to slot them into an overall category. But because alcoholism is a disease (as outlined in Chapter 1), I am certain that its victims will have little difficulty in identifying with the following pattern.

The first sign is when the individual begins to drink. In essence, if nobody drank then nobody would become an alcoholic. But this matter must be kept in perspective. The most reliable available information suggests that approximately 8–9% of all those who consume alcohol develop the condition we term 'alcoholism'. This means, of course, that the majority of drinkers do not suffer any harmful consequences, even if we allow for those problem drinkers who have not yet progressed to alcohol dependence.

BLACKOUT
The first significant sign is the occurrence of a blackout. This is a loss of memory (and not 'passing out' or 'fainting' as is sometimes wrongly believed) brought about by drink. Typically, the person concerned goes out for the evening, drinks too much, and the next day cannot remember precisely what he said or did. This places the individual on the horns of a dilemma. In the first instance he is not certain as to whether he has said or done something that merits an

apology or at least an explanation. People in this situation are also conscious of the fact that if they 'sit tight' and say nothing, they may get away with their abnormal drinking of the night before, simply by refraining from drawing attention to it.

A blackout is always of significance. This was put very neatly to me by a former patient, now happily recovered, who stated that in his drinking days somebody other than himself was writing his history. Anybody prone to blackouts would be well advised to have his drinking practices checked out and evaluated.

GULPING DRINKS

The next sign is that of 'gulping' drinks. Here the individual concerned is attempting to raise up the level of his blood alcohol as quickly as possible so that he can obtain the desired 'buzz' or 'glow' from the increased alcohol content.

In order to bring this about, the alcoholic will resort to many stratagems. At a party, he will keep constantly moving from group to group, not for reasons of sociability but in order to consume that extra drink without drawing attention to himself. Or, one may find some of the ladies retiring to the ladies' room, where they will open their handbag and surreptitiously drink the vodka or whiskey which they had earlier carefully concealed in it. Another variation is where the individual finds himself in company where the drinks are not coming up quickly enough and makes an elaborate excuse to his drinking circle, 'My word! It is now nine-thirty and I will be in hot water with the wife. Her first cousin's youngest godchild was to fly in at nine o'clock from Addis Ababa, and I was to make arrangements to meet him. I had better make a telephone call straightaway.' He then leaves the room to top up with a double in another bar in the same building. As a rule, however, alcoholics take care to ensure that they drink in the company of those who drink at the same pace as themselves.

AVOIDING THE POST-MORTEM ON THE PARTY

Associated with 'gulping drinks', is another sign. Until this phenomenon began to manifest itself, the person concerned was quite happy to have the usual post-mortem or discussion on the party that took place the night before. 'Wasn't it a great evening?' 'Wasn't it very disappointing?' 'Wasn't the supper superb?' But once the stage of gulping is reached, there is no inclination to refer to the party for the very good reason that the person concerned now feels guilty about his drinking and does not want any reminders of it.

IMPAIRED CONTROL

The next sign is probably the most significant one of all. This is what used to be referred to as 'loss of control', but more commonly these days is termed 'decreased control' or 'impaired control'. Essentially, this means that once the person concerned takes that first drink, he cannot always be certain of stopping. The key word here is *always*.

Do remember that for most of their drinking careers, alcoholics can exercise a measure of control and, indeed, will deny the existence of any problem on this ground. However, the more elderly they become, the worse their health; and above all, the more they progress in terms of their alcoholism, the less likely are they to exercise any measure of control. Hence, the ominous sayings in AA, 'For the alcoholic the first drink is the last one', or 'One drink is too many and a hundred not enough.' By contrast, the social drinker can *always* limit his intake to a fixed amount on any given occasion, if he so wills.

EXTRAVAGANCE WITH MONEY

Extravagance with money goes hand in glove with loss of control. This shows itself in many ways. In the first instance, these people will tend to spend well in excess of their income. They are inclined to 'buy the party' by paying for more than their fair share, particularly if in the company of people whom they consider to be more affluent or socially important than themselves. They often give over-generous tips or gratuities which are inappropriate for the services rendered.

One theory to account for this behaviour is that the alcoholic is attempting to expiate his guilt by subconsciously punishing himself through overspending. Whether or not

21

one subscribes to this view, the fact is that alcoholics do tend to be extravagant with money, and often at the expense of the family budget.

EXCUSES

Then there is the making of excuses, in the belief that one must do so to justify having a drink. Consider this for a moment. We live in a free society where everybody has the right to drink within the generous limits allowed by licensing laws. Logically, therefore, nobody should have to make an excuse to justify his drinking unless he happens to feel guilty over the manner of his drinking, i.e. if he is drinking abnormally.

Indeed, it never fails to astonish me that the most intelligent and sophisticated people, while in the throes of their alcoholism, will advance the most trivial of reasons to justify the taking of alcohol. For instance, if blessed with glorious, balmy spring weather this might be put forward as an excuse to have a drink on the grounds that the fine weather was coming too early in the year and we could look forward to a rainy summer! Or if, by contrast, it were cold and wet, then the taking of a drink would be rationalised by the argument that this was unseasonable weather for the time of year.

THE EARLY MORNING DRINK

An 'eye opener' is a term often used to describe taking a drink early in the morning. This is a highly significant sign and indicates that the early morning drinker is suffering from withdrawal symptoms. These commonly manifest themselves in a feeling of acute anxiety, tremors known as 'the shakes', and stomach upsets. The alcoholic suffers greatly because of these symptoms, and his early morning drinking represents an attempt to obtain relief or 'a cure' from them.

Over the years I have heard distressing accounts of people queuing up in the cold dawn for entry to the early-opening public house in the markets area of Dublin. So tremulous are some of these victims of alcohol abuse that when they are eventually served a drink they cannot hold a glass to their lips but must use a straw, or else have the glass held for them.

In our culture, this is the only sign in the field of alcoholism whose significance is rarely if ever denied or minimised. Neither should it be, as it is a positive indication of alcohol addiction in the individual displaying it.

SOLITARY DRINKING

The next sign to be considered is solitary drinking. In this context it does not mean merely taking a drink by oneself. Every day thousands of social drinkers do so and this signifies nothing sinister. However, when solitary drinking means deliberately preferring to take a drink by oneself, it is an entirely different matter. Why then should anyone seek to drink by himself? There are several explanations. In the first instance, some people may want to take a drink by themselves so that they can drink at the pace that they wish. Then too, even in these days of women's liberation many women prefer to drink secretly in order to conceal the fact that they are taking alcohol, for fear of social stigma. An important reason is that people sometimes use alcohol as a medium to escape into a world of fantasy or make-believe, where they can lead a Walter Mitty-like existence. Now in their own minds they bring off some great coups, secure a large rise in their pay packet, tell off the boss, become a great lover, poet, surgeon, architect, etc. And all this through drink! This form of solitary drinking can take place just as readily in a crowded bar or hotel lounge, as it can in the privacy of one's own room.

AGGRESSION

Aggression brought about by drinking is a common sign. It can be expressed either verbally or physically and is best divided into external or internal aggression. *External aggression* in drink is only too easy to recognise. We all know of individuals who become nasty and indulge in hurtful or malicious talk when under the influence of alcohol. Sometimes they are physically aggressive, attacking people for no good reason, or breaking up furniture, etc., and behave in a thoroughly obnoxious fashion. In some few cases, certain individuals react highly abnormally to relatively small amounts of alcohol, which bring about a change of personality with grossly out-of-character behaviour of a highly explosive and aggressive nature.

More common however, in my experience, is the *internal aggression* provoked by alcohol. Essentially, this means that the thinking of the individual becomes crooked or twisted. Exceptionally, this may manifest itself in very florid symptoms, when the drinker becomes convinced that he is the victim of some large-scale conspiracy designed to do him harm. Much more common, however, are minor forms of this reaction which cause the drinker to question the affection of his spouse, the esteem of his friends and family, and the support of colleagues and associates. I believe that the difficulties in interpersonal relationships, which are so distressing and so common in alcoholism, can nearly always be attributed to the crooked thinking of the alcoholic brought about by his abnormal drinking.

Time and again, recovered alcoholics have remarked to me how differently they view their relationships in their families, in work, or in their social lives once they have stopped drinking and begun to recover from their alcoholism. They now appreciate that the problems were fundamentally within their own minds and not due to the shortcomings of others. This improvement in interpersonal relationships is one which all recovering alcoholics can expect in due course, and is one of the really striking rewards of recovery.

'BINGE' AND 'BOUT' DRINKING

A 'binge' or 'bout' is best defined as a period of time, often lasting for several days, in which the individual drinks hopelessly and helplessly. For the duration of the 'binge' or 'bout' the alcoholic will disregard family, friends and all responsibilities in his desire to consume as much alcohol as possible. With the progression of the disease, the interval between 'bouts' may become shorter, and the duration of the 'bouts' longer, until the alcoholic's tolerance for alcohol decreases to the stage where it becomes apparent that he can no longer consume it on the same scale as before.

In many cases, 'bout' or 'binge' drinking is linked with depression or, less commonly, elation. When a careful history is taken, the pattern of going on 'binges' or 'bouts' in response to seasonal swings of mood becomes apparent. Often these mood swings occur in spring or autumn with the turn of the leaf, and coincide with the alcoholic's spring or autumn 'binges' or 'bouts' which his family has learned to anticipate and dread. Vigorous prophylactic and therapeutic measures designed to deal with the mood swings can usually abort the 'binge' or 'bout' when it is linked to these depressions and elations.

REMORSE-RESENTMENT

The next phase is that of remorse. After the 'binge' or 'bout', alcoholics suffer a great deal. They often feel physically sick and are tremulous, their mind is in a turmoil and, above all, they are racked with guilt and haunted by self-reproach. They are only too well aware of having been warned of the danger in taking those first few drinks, and are tortured by disappointment at having succumbed to temptation, thereby putting their hard won sobriety in jeopardy.

But when they feel better, they begin to think differently and attempt to analyse the reasons for their relapse. 'The wife/husband or family had not been very supportive of late.' 'My friends don't seem to bother with me any more.' 'My workmates/boss are imposing on me just because I've a drink problem.' 'I recently met my doctor who seems to have lost interest in me.' And now they press the argument further! It is the fault of their husband, wife or family, their friends, workmates/boss or doctor. They are then filled with a resentment towards these people whom they blame for their relapse.

DEEP NAMELESS ANXIETY

Deep nameless anxiety, brought about by drink, is a highly unpleasant symptom of alcoholism. This reaction is much more than the ordinary feelings of anxiety which all of us experience from time to time. Here, the man or woman affected is deeply troubled by a sense of impending doom. Their stomachs churn over, their pulses race and they tend to sweat excessively. The only solution to their predicament, as they see it, is to look for a drink. Should they be in a situation where drink is not readily available, their symptoms intensify. Accordingly, they try to ensure that alcohol is always

25

readily available to them, even if it means concealing bottles in toilet cisterns, under the mattress, in closets, or wherever. I remember well the chagrin of a farmer who was treated successfully some years ago when, following his return home, he came across bottles of whiskey concealed in hiding places all over the farm. He had put them there while troubled by deep nameless anxiety during his drinking days, but could not remember their exact location due to the blackouts which he experienced regularly. This man felt even more mortified when his family and farmhands located the bottles of whiskey which he had, as he thought, carefully concealed in sheds, ditches, etc.

GETTING HELP IN A CRISIS

At the next stage the alcoholic gets help. Immediately, this poses the question, 'Why?' To answer this comprehensively would take a long time and involve a great deal of speculation and much theorising. Let me generalise and state that the reason why the alcoholic seeks help is because of some crisis in his life. This is very apparent in cases where the wife or husband declares, 'Unless you go for treatment I will leave you', or the boss states that the alcoholic's job is lost unless he or she submit themselves to a course of treatment.

How fortunate are those victims of alcohol who are afforded help with their alcoholism before they have suffered unduly and have been spared many of the humiliations which are part and parcel of the consequences of alcohol abuse. Such people should take advantage of their good fortune and avail to the full of the help being offered to them. Never forget that alcoholism is a progressive disease. The only time to do something about it is *now*!

Also, do remember that the majority of alcoholics who are exposed to a modern, properly mounted treatment programme, benefit considerably from it. Those who comply best will do best.

SKID ROW

The last stage is where the alcoholic reaches 'skid row' as traditionally defined. At this juncture, the alcoholic has lost family, friends and fortune because of drink, and is reduced to living the life of a vagrant. Fortunately, only some 6% of the alcoholic population are eventually reduced to this condition according to some authorities.

Sometimes we hear it stated that the alcoholic cannot be helped unless he reaches 'skid row'. This is heresy — dangerous heresy — because of the progressive nature of alcoholism. Alcoholics all too often meet with severe misfortune in different guises and, unfortunately, die prematurely from accidents, overdoses, heart attacks, etc. To stand idly by rather than intervene professionally is to run the very real risk of allowing the alcoholic to do himself serious harm in many areas of his life. To my mind the concept of a 'personal skid row' is a much more valid one when it comes to helping the alcoholic. This term means that the individual has reached a stage in his life, when his circumstances are so unacceptable to him because of his drinking habits, that he is now amenable to constructive advice and help. The key word is 'personal'. For example, to some alcoholics the loss of the affection of their spouse might be crucial, while this fact might mean little to others. Inability to perform their job to the best of their capabilities might weigh heavily with some, but might be of little consequence to others.

In my experience a great many alcoholics will eventually seek help because of this personal 'skid row'. Quite often, their reasons for looking for help are hard to comprehend, when viewed in the context of the history of the alcoholic in question. That is why a sympathetic and understanding approach to the alcoholic must be maintained at all times, so that when they reach their 'personal skid row' they will turn to the individual who showed understanding, and now accept advice and assistance. This is yet another example of the necessity for patience and persistence in the treatment of alcoholism.

Cross Addiction

This is a matter of constant concern for those of us working in the field of alcohol abuse or alcoholism. Essentially, cross addiction means that the individual who has become addicted to or dependent on any one substance is much more at risk of becoming dependent on other substances than is the non-addict. In practical terms, if somebody has become dependent on alcohol then he is much more at risk of becoming dependent on some other substance than is the ordinary social drinker.

In many of the USA alcohol treatment centres a significant proportion of the clients presenting for treatment have a dependency on narcotics as well as on alcohol. They are termed 'poly abusers'.

In Ireland, this particular problem is not yet as common as in the USA. Rather, we are usually concerned with the abuse of tranquillisers and sleeping tablets and, to a lesser degree, of anti-depressants and pep pills on the part of alcoholics. This has provoked an over-reaction in some quarters, resulting in the sweeping statement often forcefully expressed that no alcoholic should ever take drugs.

One of the difficulties here is that the term 'drug' is a highly emotive one. Very often the distinction between narcotic drugs such as heroin, 'crack', etc. and prescribed drugs is blurred, and the tendency is to equate one with the other. For this reason it is advisable to use the term medication when describing prescribed drugs. I believe too that the taking of medication by the alcoholic must be put into proper perspective. It is just as absurd to state categorically that alcoholics should never use medication as it would be to postulate that all alcoholics should be prescribed medication. The basic difficulty here is a tendency to confuse the proper use of medication with its abuse. So, too, the ordinary social drinker makes proper use of alcohol while the alcoholic abuses it. It does not follow, however, that the sale or use of alcohol should be proscribed.

Medication, carefully prescribed, is sometimes necessary for alcoholics. An instance is the short-term use of tranquillisers in detoxification. Anti-depressants are highly efficacious in the case of alcoholics subject to depression, a relatively common associated condition which must be vigorously treated to enable the alcoholic to come to terms with his alcoholism.

In my experience, if two basic rules are observed in respect of the use of medication by the alcoholic, the risk of cross addiction can be virtually discounted.

In the first instance, an alcoholic should take a prescription only from a doctor who is familiar with his history. One often hears criticism, unfortunately sometimes justified, of doctors being too liberal in their prescribing of medication. It must be remembered, however, that most practising doctors are busy people and, with the pressures of a heavy case load, may be manipulated by a plausible alcoholic into issuing a prescription which they would not do were they aware of the history of the individual concerned. The second rule is very basic. The instructions on the prescription should be followed precisely and exactly. If the patient has any doubts about the type of medication or dosage prescribed, then he should contact the doctor who issued the prescription and make his reservations known to him. In this way the doctor concerned will be enabled to refine his prescription in a manner which will be more beneficial to the patient. The danger here is that of consulting a friend or acquaintance who may turn out to be a pundit.

In Ireland, pundits abound. I define them as individuals whose readiness to pontificate on a subject is in inverse proportion to their knowledge of the subject concerned. The world of alcoholism has a fascination for pundits, sometimes masquerading as self-declared experts in the field. The use of medication is all too often the subject of their most sweeping assertions, notwithstanding the fact that only doctors are licensed in law to prescribe medication, and have to undertake the responsibility to do so competently and properly, or else run the risk of medico-legal consequences. That said, I hold the view that it is not necessary for the majority of alcoholics to take medication in the long term.

Discussion

(a) *Must one have experienced all of the signs and symptoms to be diagnosed an alcoholic?*
This is not necessary. The pattern set out is that of the 'average alcoholic', a term which is merely a statistical convenience. One need not experience all the signs and symptoms, or indeed, in the sequence set out, to be deemed a sufferer from alcoholism. However, I believe that anybody with an

alcoholic problem, will readily identify with the pattern which I have just described — provided they take a clear and objective view of their drinking history, and keep an open mind when looking at the pattern.

(b) *Could one be an alcoholic without ever taking a drink, i.e. could one be said to be born an alcoholic?*
Alcoholism can only be diagnosed on the consideration of abnormal drinking. Therefore, if one never takes a drink one can never be diagnosed as an alcoholic. We now know that those individuals with a loaded family history of alcoholism are more at risk than those people coming from families with little or no alcoholism. Nevertheless, irrespective of background, only those people who consume alcohol can be taken into account when it comes to making a diagnosis of alcoholism.

(c) *'For many years, my tolerance for alcohol was considerable. Latterly it appears to have decreased dramatically.' Does this happen to many alcoholics?*
What is described here is very common. Some people are born with a high tolerance for alcohol. More important however in the development of tolerance is continuous drinking, or what the Americans quaintly term as 'training'. Accordingly, most alcoholics develop a high tolerance which usually persists for a considerable period of time. With the progression of the alcoholism, the stage is reached where the tolerance drops — often quite suddenly. Now the alcoholic finds himself in the position where it is apparent that he is under the influence, by contrast with the situation which obtained for many years when he could get away, so to speak, with taking a great many drinks: 'For years I could go out at night and polish off my full quota of drinks with the lads and return home without the wife being suspicious. Now I am spotted if I take only one or two drinks.'

(d) *If someone is addicted to sleeping pills, should they take a drink?*
The prudent course for such a person would be to abstain from alcohol until they are certain that they have rid themselves of their addiction to their sleeping pills.

(e) *If a person takes two or three double whiskeys, for example, every night before he retires, is he an alcoholic?*

The diagnosis of alcoholism is a serious matter, and should never be lightly made without careful consideration of all the facts, as outlined. See Chapter 1, Discussion (c).

(f) *Is the keeping of a 'drinking diary' recommended?*

This can be very helpful if accurate information is consistently recorded.

(g) *Is gambling sometimes associated with alcoholism?*

Yes, and often because of the compulsive nature of the individual concerned. A successful recovery from the alcoholism is essential if the gambling problem is to be overcome.

4

From Compulsion to Recovery

Compulsion

The question of a compulsion to drink, or having a craving
for alcohol, is obviously central to the problem of alcohol
abuse or alcoholism. In many cases it is advanced by the
alcoholic as a reason for failure to stop drinking, or for a
relapse. The following attempts to explain the nature of
compulsion.

This theory is based on a simple experiment. The scientists
concerned put a small dog into a cage and left the animal
without food. After a time, the dog became hungry and
anxious and began to pace restlessly round and round the
cage. In so doing, he hit against a lever projecting from the
side of the cage and thereby discharged a portion of food
which fell into the cage. The animal ate this food with alacrity
and so relieved his hunger and diminished his anxiety.

This experiment was repeated a number of times. Eventually, depending on his intelligence, the dog learned to
associate the pressing of the lever with the gaining of food
and the diminution of anxiety.

The results of this experiment were transposed to the
human situation. It is now postulated that the alcoholic has
learned, over the years, to associate the act of drinking with
relief of tension and diminution of anxiety. For him, going
into the pub, smelling the cigarette smoke, listening to the
hubbub of conversation, looking at the lights shining on the
bottles; or locking the door of the sitting-room, checking to
ensure that he is unobserved, retrieving the bottle from its
hiding place — all of these factors are part and parcel of the

tried and trusted ritual which will invariably produce short-term relief of anxiety. The feel of the glass on the lips, the sensation of the drink hitting the stomach: taken together with the sedative effect of the alcohol, all add to the attraction of drinking for the alcoholic.

And then, in the case of the alcoholic, because his body has become sensitised to alcohol, once he has taken that first drink the tissues of his body cry out for more and more, until the alcoholic finds that he cannot control the amount of alcohol he consumes. 'One drink is too many, one hundred not enough.'

In essence then, the alcoholic takes that first drink in response to stress, having learned from long experience that this will give quick relief. With the passage of time, the occasions of stress will become more numerous, until the alcoholic will sometimes subconsciously reach for a drink because of what appears to the ordinary social drinker to be a very trivial reason indeed. This reaction is in line with the low frustration threshold which is so evident in many persons prone to alcoholism.

The Management of Alcoholism

There are two primary problems where the management of alcoholism is concerned.

ACCEPTANCE OF DIAGNOSIS

The basic question that comes to mind — considering the individual's reluctance so often to agree with this diagnosis — is: what makes the idea so unacceptable? After all, in the ordinary way, if a patient goes along to consult a doctor, once the history is taken and the carrying out of the examination and certain investigations are completed, in most instances the patient is prepared to accept the diagnosis. They may not be pleased to be informed that they are suffering from emphysema or osteo-arthritis for instance, but this will not prevent them from accepting the diagnosis, as is so often the case when alcoholism is diagnosed.

One factor is the loss of self esteem the patient suffers if he agrees with the diagnosis and then continues to drink.

As long as he denies the disease, he ostensibly preserves his status as a non-alcoholic and has no real reason to abstain, except temporarily.

One may well ask, how can somebody displaying many or most of the signs and symptoms outlined in Chapter 3 possibly deny the diagnosis? Surely the man prone to blackouts or aggressive behaviour following a drinking episode, cannot run away from the possibility that he may be suffering from alcohol dependence? And yet this reaction is all too common. It is brought about by the individual concerned taking one sign or symptom which he lacks, and claiming that since this is essential to the diagnosis, his lack of it automatically excludes him. For instance, the individual who drinks in bars says, 'I never drink alone.' The man who drinks alone states, 'I never drink in the morning.'

But if the individual goes on to agree that he is an alcoholic and then continues to drink, now in effect he is admitting that he has lost control over his intake — literally that he must have alcohol in excess in order to continue to function.

Such an admission destroys much of the rationalisation system. Their endlessly repeated assurances to the family, 'If my drinking gets any worse, I'll do something about it', or the classical one, 'I can take it or leave it alone', cease to make any sense, even to themselves. It is generally agreed that the alcoholic cannot take it or leave it alone. If he agrees that he is an alcoholic, there is no need to delay treatment until things get worse. The term implies that things are already at their worst.

This is a response with which I am all too familiar in my work. Regularly I am asked to see somebody who has been abusing alcohol, and after a preliminary examination inform him that I believe him to have a drinking problem. Quite often I am met with a flat denial, 'Doctor, I'm afraid you do not understand the position. Things have been very bad with me in recent months, but thankfully, there has been a great improvement in my fortunes of late. I'm quite certain that I will now be able to drink normally.' And then there ensues a dialogue, often ending in a compromise, where the individual puts off coming for full assessment and treatment, but agrees to do so should his drinking get out of hand.

Almost invariably, because of the progressive nature of alcoholism, the position will deteriorate and the alcoholic will find himself forced to accept treatment, but on much more disadvantageous terms, having suffered considerably in the interim, than if they had taken the advice offered in the first instance. The hard fact is that the only time for the alcoholic to have treatment is *now* — otherwise the alcoholic and everybody connected with him will be subject to a great deal of additional suffering.

Another factor in the reluctance to agree with the diagnosis is that, while most diagnoses are regarded as impersonal names for unfortunate events which may occur to anybody, alcoholism is an exception. Even today, when there is so much more understanding of the alcoholism — thanks to a great extent to the acceptance of the disease concept — a stigma, nevertheless, still attaches to the condition.

The term alcoholic is one which still gives rise to considerable misunderstanding and hinders the acceptance of the diagnosis. It is commonly used in a very loose fashion and thrown around as freely as 'snuff at a wake'. Too often it is employed in a pejorative sense. 'What else could you expect of Mick, he is only an alcoholic.' And yet, if one challenges the individual making this judgment to define the term 'alcoholic', nearly always he will fail to do so accurately. This is why I find it so necessary to be certain when using the term 'alcoholic' that those with whom I am conversing hold to the same definition as I do myself. As stated in Chapter 1, I use the working definition advanced by Marty Mann many years ago: 'An alcoholic is anybody whose drinking causes a continuing problem in any area of their lives.' You will note that this is a non-judgmental definition, which certainly does not attempt to classify the alcoholic as somebody suffering from a character disorder or personality defect.

This then brings us to the nub of the problem where acceptance of the diagnosis is concerned. Since the alcoholic is himself a member of the responsive public which does not always accept alcoholism as a disease, but rather views it as a character defect or moral weakness, the alcoholic inevitably shares this general derogatory view of the condition, and for most of his drinking career may refuse to apply it to himself.

The education of the general public in respect of the disease concept of alcoholism, and a widespread acceptance that the alcoholic is as deserving of the same support and understanding as the victim of any other disease, is essential if the alcoholic and his family are to be persuaded to accept the diagnosis. Indeed, a reappraisal of the entire question of alcohol abuse and the place of alcohol in our society would be highly pertinent at the present time.

ACCEPTANCE OF TREATMENT

Obviously, if the patient persists in denying the diagnosis, there is no *internal* reason for accepting treatment. Although he may reluctantly agree to a consultation under pressure exerted by spouse, family or employer, it can be anticipated that when these external forces abate, so will the patient's interest in treatment. Note the importance of the word 'internal'.

Let me put the matter in practical terms. Every year a large number of people are admitted to psychiatric hospitals for the treatment of alcoholism. Something in excess of 90% of the total come in as voluntary patients, in the technical meaning of the term. That is to say, they sign a piece of paper affirming that they wish to enter the hospital concerned as a voluntary patient. By so doing, they conform with the regulations which govern the admission of non-certified patients to all psychiatric hospitals throughout the Republic of Ireland.

However, I have often speculated as to how many of this large number are truly voluntary admissions in the ordinary meaning of the term 'voluntary'. How many of them come in entirely freely of their own accord? I am certain that if the matter were examined in detail one would find the percentage would drop down very sharply indeed. In many cases admission is brought about by outside pressures. The wife/husband says, 'Look, I've had enough. Unless you go for treatment, I will leave you.' The boss declares, 'Your job is gone unless you have a course of treatment', or the judge states, 'Go into hospital for treatment or I'll be forced to imprison you.' In the great majority of cases, as soon as the alcoholic commences to think clearly following detoxification, he appreciates that he is in a caring atmosphere where expert help is available, and meets up with a variety of people with the same problem. He is now happy to apply himself to the treatment programme with varying degrees of commitment.

In a small number of cases the alcoholic cannot be persuaded to do so at this juncture in his life. This is of course most unfortunate as it means, as I have attempted to stress, that some crisis or catastrophe will have to ensue before he is prepared to accept help. Very exceptionally, the individual may be so resentful of having been pressurised to come into hospital that he will attempt to sabotage the treatment programme. This rare occurrence is totally unacceptable lest it should interfere, even to a limited extent, with the recovery of other alcoholic patients, all of whom are the victims of a killing disease. I emphasise this point, knowing only too well just how difficult it can be for some individuals to come to terms with the diagnosis and treatment of alcoholism. This is why it is necessary to adopt a patient but persistent and firm approach to alcoholic patients in accordance with the treatment philosophy, which recognises that no alcoholic consciously sets out to develop the condition, but insists that he takes the primary responsibility for his recovery, once the condition is diagnosed, and its implications explained to the individual alcoholic.

But now we have to ask a fundamental question. What does treatment mean to the alcoholic, compared with medical treatment in general? In most sickness, treatment implies relief, and the more effective the treatment, the more obvious and prolonged the relief.

Let us take the case of a man stricken with pneumonia, in order to illustrate the point. The two distressing symptoms in this condition are pain in the chest because of the associated pleurisy, and shortness of breath. As soon as a doctor is called on to treat a case of pneumonia, he will straightaway administer a pain-killing drug to ease the chest pain and also an antibiotic which will relieve the difficulty in breathing. The patient will now readily equate treatment with relief from his distressing symptoms and is therefore only too happy to accept the treatment regime.

But not so with alcoholism. All worthwhile forms of treatment for alcoholism begin with taking alcohol away from the alcoholic. He may very often perceive treatment as a deprivation which he fears he will be unable to endure. In his mind, effective treatment may imply the permanent loss of the substance which, for him, apparently is life's most precious offering. For this reason, some patients will sacrifice spouse, family and job rather than seriously considering giving up alcohol.

The fundamental point here, and one which is not appreciated nearly as much as it should be, is that alcohol for the alcoholic is the most important thing in his life. How often have I heard exasperated family members expostulate, 'Why can't Mick think rationally as I do?' 'Why can't he curb his drinking or confine it to beer, wine, etc.?' The very basic answer is that Mick suffers from alcoholism. The frustrated individual asking the question does not, and cannot comprehend just how much alcohol means to Mick, and the extent to which it has come to dominate his life. If the answer to alcoholism was merely to give up alcohol, then it would not be the massive problem that it is today. I am convinced that often too much emphasis is placed on the necessity for the alcoholic to stop drinking, rather than looking on this measure as a means towards the goal of treatment: *recovery*. The objective of any worthwhile treatment programme is much more than merely taking alcohol away from the alcoholic, which is in essence a negative approach. Rather, the aim is to bring alcoholic patients to the stage of recovery through sobriety. Not for a moment do I concede that anything short of total sobriety is essential for recovery in the case of the alcoholic. Nevertheless, all alcoholics, and in particular those exposed for the first time to a treatment programme, should be aware that its objective is recovery rather than mere abstinence.

RECOVERY

Recovery, as I see it, has two components. The first is 'liberation'. This may sound over-dramatic, but I make no apology for using the term because it is so true in this context. No alcoholic is a free man, because his life is governed by drink. Indeed, particularly in the case of women alcoholics, their lives are controlled by other people because of their dependence on alcohol. Recovery means freedom to live, or lead whatever kind of life one chooses, having rid oneself of the domination of alcohol.

The second component is 'restoration' to health and peace of mind. Alcoholics suffer far more than social drinkers from a wide variety of physical and psychiatric complications, a fact demonstrated in numerous studies conducted in treatment centres throughout the western world, and confirmed by research carried out on a large sample of Irish alcoholics in the late 1970s. Accordingly, alcoholics can anticipate an improvement in their health with the attainment of recovery. They will also experience *peace of mind*. During their drinking days, alcoholics are racked with guilt arising out of their lying, manipulations, etc. As soon as they begin to recover, the need for deception is removed and a large load lifted from them.

Let me stress that recovery does not come overnight. Patience and persistence with the aftercare programme are essential for its attainment. Be assured, however, that recovery is within the reach of every alcoholic *in due course*, save for the exceptional few who are afflicted with gross brain damage.

So when one thinks of treatment, concentrate on recovery and the rewards of sobriety, instead of being preoccupied with the ordeal of giving up drink. Take heart from the numbers of people, now well advanced in their recovery, who not so long ago at the commencement of their treatment programme were assailed by the same misgivings and apprehensions.

The successful utilisation of the factors or forces within oneself is the key to recovery and will always prevail, no matter what external pressures may manifest themselves.

Discussion

(a) *In the public mind there does not appear to be any distinction made between 'the drinking alcoholic' and 'the recovered alcoholic', with both parties labelled as alcoholics in an indiscriminate way. Does this create problems?*

Yes it does, in many cases. The failure to distinguish between those suffering from alcoholism who have recovered from the condition, and the victims of the disease who have not come to terms with it, is yet another indication of the lack of understanding of alcoholism which still prevails. Thankfully the position is improving all the time, in large measure because of the many alcoholics who regularly attain the goal of recovery and by so doing demonstrate the fundamental distinction between the recovered alcoholic and the drinking alcoholic.

(b) *How can the alcoholic look for a drink to relieve stress, knowing that the next day he is going to be sick, miserable and tormented with guilt after his lapse?*
The alcoholic confronted with a stressful situation is concerned only with *immediate relief.* He is not bothered about tomorrow. This does not enter into his thoughts. This view is typical of the alcoholic's mentality during his drinking days.

(c) *Does the compulsion to drink abate or disappear with recovery?*
We know that in general terms the longer an alcoholic is 'on the dry', the less likely is he to be troubled by a compulsion to drink. This is a fact which should encourage every alcoholic, and in particular those at the early stages of recovery. In more scientific terms, if a response is not reinforced, as happens when the compulsion to drink is not gratified, it will eventually become extinct.

(d) *Why are more people coming forward for treatment?*
The fact that so many more people now come forward for treatment is, in my opinion, due to the increasing enlightenment which prevails here in Ireland. However, the position is still well removed from being entirely satisfactory. I am certain that the demonstrable recovery of so many victims of alcoholism in every walk of Irish life, has been the single most important factor in improving the public understanding of alcoholism.

5

Physical and Psychiatric Complications

ALCOHOL affects every system of the body. In recent years, medical literature has highlighted this fact by drawing attention to the part played by alcohol in medical conditions, where the connection with alcohol intake was formerly either ignored or understated. The complications I shall discuss are those seen regularly in patients presenting for treatment.

It is certainly not my intention to scare anybody when I outline the different complications, if only because experience has brought home to me that such an approach is rarely effective in the long term and, indeed, can be counterproductive in persuading the alcoholic to give up drink as the first essential step to recovery. 'Doctor, if my liver is that bad, then there is little prospect of my living a long life, so I may as well enjoy what time is left for me and drink all I can.'

It is, however, essential to make known to alcoholic patients the risks that they take in respect of their health if they continue to drink in the face of medical advice. This of course is in line with the basic philosophy of treatment, which states clearly that each alcoholic must assume the primary responsibility for his recovery, and take full advantage of all the help and assistance which is readily available for themselves and their families.

The complications brought about by alcohol abuse can best be described by placing them within the different systems of the body.

Digestive

The tongue of the alcoholic frequently becomes red, cracked and sore. The reason for this change is the shortage of vitamins, in particular those of the vitamin B group, commonly experienced by alcoholics. This is due to two factors. In the first place, alcoholics do not eat very well: 'Why waste valuable drinking time on food?' Consequently they do not take enough vitamins for their ordinary needs. Furthermore, they require extra vitamin B because of their increased alcohol intake, a fact which aggravates the vitamin shortage. The condition of the tongue is an example of this avitaminosis.

Gastritis is another complication. This can be due to many causes, as is the case with some of the other complications which I shall discuss. In all instances I shall of course be referring only to those where alcohol is the primary cause of the condition described.

The term 'gastritis' describes an inflammation of the lining of the stomach. This is aggravated by the shortage of vitamins to which I referred earlier and also, according to some authorities, by the mechanical action of the alcohol hitting against the delicate stomach lining. The condition gives rise to a very common symptom: distaste for food, particularly early in the morning. In its extreme form this results in distressing dry retching when the affected individual cannot bear the sight or smell of food, much less contemplate having breakfast. Let me emphasise that gastritis, as well as the condition of the tongue, are both reversible, provided the sufferer is prepared to stop drinking and take the appropriate treatment. In practical terms I have been impressed over the years with the number of alcoholic patients who volunteered the statement to me after the first ten or twelve days of treatment: 'Doctor, already I feel so much better. I now find that for the first time in years I can eat a cooked breakfast.'

LIVER

We now come to consider the damage caused to the liver, the largest organ in the body and the one notoriously affected by excessive intake of alcohol.

The mildest liver condition brought about by excessive drinking is the development of 'fatty liver' where some of the normal liver cells are replaced by globules of fat. This means that the liver can no longer function efficiently, and this leads to a deterioration of the general health of the individual affected.

Hepatitis or inflammation of the liver is a much more serious complication. Again let me stress that we are concerned with hepatitis brought about through drink. Virus hepatitis is very much in the news these days, but this is a different matter. Those affected by alcoholic hepatitis become quite ill and may be jaundiced. They require specialist medical treatment which is highly effective in bringing about recovery.

The most extreme form of liver disease is of course cirrhosis or scarring of the liver. This is most commonly found in daily drinkers who rarely give their livers an opportunity to rest and recover from the onslaught of alcohol. Cirrhosis is also more common in women alcoholics. It is a very serious complication with grave, long-term implications. However, thanks to the advances of modern medical practice, the outlook is much more hopeful these days provided the alcoholic is prepared to become a teetotaller. Do remember that cirrhosis of the liver is not invariably due to alcohol. The existence of juvenile cirrhosis of the liver proves the point.

CANCER

At this juncture we must face up to a very serious consequence of excessive drinking. I refer of course to cancer, in particular cancer of the back of the mouth, throat, gullet and bowel. Among alcoholics there is a well documented increase in the incidence of cancer in these sites.

RESPIRATORY

Next we must consider the respiratory system which has to do with our breathing. Many alcoholics suffer from bronchitis. One of my pet theories is that anybody with an alcohol problem who is subject to bronchitis, can expect a bonus in the form of a marked improvement in their bronchitis, provided they are prepared to stop drinking. This has been borne home to me over the years from listening to the many alcoholic patients subject to bronchitis who say to me: 'Doctor, I feel so well since I stopped drinking. It's the first time for years that I have not been coughing and hawking up sputum, that I have been able to give up antibiotics, that I no longer dread the winter months.'

In the old days many alcoholics died from *pneumonia*. Since the discovery of antibiotics, this is no longer the case. Do remember, however, that pneumonia is still a serious condition because of its residual effects on the heart, kidneys, etc.

HEART

For many years past, since the days when the condition of 'Munich Beer Heart' among the heavy-drinking brewery workers in that city was described, doctors have been only too well aware that excessive drinking damages the heart. This is brought about by the toxic effects of alcohol on the heart muscle, and compounded by the lack of vitamin B common in alcohol abusers. The heart muscle is damaged to the extent that it can no longer function efficiently. The consequence is that the blood tends to pool in the ankles, or at the base of the lungs, and heart failure is now apparent.

Excessive drinking tends to produce a rise in *blood pressure*. Quite often abstinence brings about an appreciable fall in blood pressure readings, even in cases which have proved intractable to standard medical treatments.

BRAIN DAMAGE

In recent years there has been considerable concern expressed about the association between brain damage and alcohol. Coarse brain damage is the equivalent of what in AA circles is termed 'wet brain'. Here, large tracts of the brain are destroyed by alcohol. It is not a common complication, which is just as well because the consequences are very serious indeed.

Thanks to the advances in diagnostic procedures, we now know that mild brain damage due to alcoholism is much more common than was formerly suspected. The verbal skills of those afflicted by mild brain damage are usually preserved intact, but their performance ability suffers. This is why it is sometimes difficult to diagnose the condition, particularly if the individual affected is well educated and fluent with words. Let me stress the heartening fact that if these people abstain from alcohol their outlook is good; they will be able to compensate quite readily for their brain damage as they advance on the road to recovery.

44

NERVOUS SYSTEM

The effects of excessive drinking are many and varied in this system.

Peripheral neuritis is a common complication. This means that the nerves of the feet, legs, hands and arms are damaged by drink, producing a loss of feeling in the extremities of the body where a tingling sensation will persist. In addition, the ability to carry out fine movements with one's hands, or to walk consistently in a straight line, may be impaired. That is why the victim of peripheral neuritis frequently fumbles when attempting to button his jacket, to take a common example. The encouraging fact is that peripheral neuritis is eminently treatable, provided the individual affected gives up alcohol and takes large doses of vitamin B.

PSYCHIATRIC

Paranoid states brought about by alcohol intake are much more common than is generally realised, particularly in the milder forms. A distressing example is morbid jealousy. Gross paranoid reactions where there are marked persecutory delusions are readily recognisable but fortunately are rare. So common are mild paranoid states, and so devastating are their effects on interpersonal relationships, that they need to be highlighted much more, particularly in view of the great improvement which abstinence brings about.

WITHDRAWAL STATE

Perhaps the most striking complication in respect of the nervous system is the development of the withdrawal state. Paradoxically, this is directly due to the lack of alcohol, and manifests itself commonly two to six days after the last drink. Signs and symptoms vary in degree from feelings of anxiety and a mild degree of shakiness up to delirium tremens or DTs. Here, the alcoholic is confused in respect of time, place and person. He may suffer from visual hallucinations when all sorts of imaginary objects and creatures appear to be threatening him as he lies helpless in bed in a state of terror. Sometimes, he is deluded to the extent that he believes he is following his normal occupation. Many years ago we had referred to us for treatment a celebrated chef who developed

DTs shortly after coming into hospital. I well remember sitting by his bedside and being fascinated listening to him giving orders to his assistants, in the belief that he was still presiding over his kitchens like the maestro that he was. It was quite intriguing to hear the poor man instruct his team to attend to the wishes of the notables who patronised the restaurant, and to hear him name some of the well-known personalities of the day.

Delirium tremens is a very serious and life-threatening condition. One of the standard textbooks on psychiatry states bluntly that the mortality rate is in the order of 16%. In a properly run detoxification unit, however, the mortality rate is almost zero. I make this point to emphasise that withdrawing a patient from alcohol, particularly if he is elderly, in poor physical health or advanced in his alcoholism, can be a hazardous procedure, and should only be undertaken in a setting where expert medical and nursing care are available, together with the necessary facilities.

That said, I should point out that these days we do not see nearly as many cases of DTs as we did some fifteen or twenty years ago. This appears to be the position also in treatment centres in other countries. Why this change has come about is far from clear.

FITS

Sometimes the withdrawal state may manifest itself in the form of epileptic fits. Quite regularly, middle-aged men are brought to the casualty department of hospitals following an epileptic fit. Straightaway an intensive search is instituted for a brain tumour, metabolic disease, etc. It is only when elaborate investigations fail to turn up any finding of consequence that the drinking history is scrutinised. The patient now volunteers the information that he had become concerned over the pattern of his drinking and stopped abruptly. Three days later he developed the fit which led to his hospitalisation.

Patients suffering from DTs are prone to chest infections which may progress to full-blown pneumonia. Should this occur, then the doctor responsible for the patient will have a very sick individual on his hands. The survival of the patient will depend on the level of medical and nursing expertise which can be mobilised.

BLINDNESS

Blindness due to drink is caused by the ingestion of crude alcohol. Some years ago there was a scare in Connemara when the local poteen (poitín)-maker or moonshiner got his formula wrong and his clients wound up in Galway Regional Hospital suffering from blindness. Fortunately it was of a temporary nature. Sometimes, however, it can be permanent when the optic nerve, or nerve of sight, at the back of the eyeball is so badly damaged by crude alcohol that recovery is not possible.

AUDITORY HALLUCINATIONS

The development of auditory hallucinations is a distressing complication. Here the individual concerned is going around topped up with alcohol to the extent that one would never suspect that he had drink taken, but all the time he is hearing imaginary voices saying such obscene or horrifying things to him, that he becomes acutely anxious. This leads him to take more and more alcohol in an attempt to obtain relief, until he eventually collapses.

THE KORSAKOFF STATE

The Korsakoff state is a complication of chronic alcoholism. Every psychiatric hospital in this country has several long-stay patients suffering from the Korsakoff state. Its outstanding characteristic is the loss of memory for recent events, while by contrast that for the past is surprisingly intact. It is sometimes difficult to recognise this fact as these people become expert at covering up this deficit, i.e. confabulation. Their mood is unstable so that they can change quite suddenly from a rather inane euphoria to outright aggression, for no apparent reason. Quite often they are bothered by severe peripheral neuritis to the extent that they experience pain in their limbs. There is no cure for the Korsakoff state, which is why these victims of chronic alcoholism have to be maintained in sheltered care, as they are incapable of looking after themselves or their affairs.

The last complication which I will now outline is a grim one, but must be faced as it is all too common. I refer, of course, to premature death.

Anybody involved in the treatment of those who abuse alcohol as well as alcoholics over a period of time, will be only too well aware of the disturbingly high numbers who meet with untimely deaths due to accidents, burning, choking on their vomit, heart attacks, over-dosing both accidental and deliberate, etc. Moreover studies here in Ireland have confirmed quite clearly the harsh fact revealed by similar enquiries in other countries that the rate of suicide is greatly increased among alcoholics.

Let me conclude as I started, by reiterating that the detailed recital of this formidable list of complications is not intended to upset or frighten, but to emphasise the risks to health brought about by excessive drinking. Do bear in mind that most of the complications can be successfully treated if the individual concerned is prepared to abstain from alcohol and to co-operate with treatment.

Discussion

(a) *Surely the fact that so many alcoholics smoke a great deal must have something to do with the high rate of bronchitis in alcoholics?*
This is true. Nevertheless, even if the recovered alcoholic continues to smoke, his bronchitis will certainly improve because of his continuing sobriety.

(b) *Can the tissues of the brain recover from the damage caused by alcohol?*
The standard medical answer has always been *no* and this is still the case. However, the results of recent research have indicated that the traditional medical view may need to be revised.

(c) *Many of the complications associated with alcohol abuse can be reversed on the basis of sobriety. How true is this statement?*
Nearly all the common complications can be relieved to a significant extent, provided that those affected give up drink.

The outlook is much better than many might believe if they were to listen to the misleading tales of doom and gloom which are all too prevalent in the field of alcohol abuse.

(d) *Does alcoholism progress during sobriety?*

No, save in the rare enough event of some organ being so damaged by alcohol that it does not recover even when the alcoholic achieves sobriety.

The reason however for the view that alcoholism progresses during sobriety is bound up with tolerance for alcohol. As I have indicated on page 30(c) the principal factor in the development of tolerance is drinking practice or 'training', so to speak. If a person commences to drink again after a period of sobriety, he cannot now handle alcohol as before, and may arrive at the erroneous conclusion that his alcoholism had progressed during his sobriety.

6

Antabuse in the Treatment of Alcoholism

MANY YEARS ago, it was accidentally discovered that the substance Antabuse had the peculiar property of making anyone who took it sensitive to drink. It was found that the consumption of alcohol, after taking Antabuse, produced a flushing of the face, palpitations, a constriction in the chest, nausea sometimes leading to vomiting, together with a fall in blood pressure. Collectively, these symptoms constitute what is termed an Antabuse reaction. The severity of an Antabuse reaction depends on three factors: the dosage of the Antabuse, the amount of alcohol consumed and, most important of all, the reaction of the individual concerned.

In the past, it was the practice to expose those alcoholics considered suitable for Antabuse therapy to a test beforehand. They were given a tablet of Antabuse followed by a bottle of beer. It was found that occasionally one of those tested in this manner suffered a severe reaction, even though he had taken the same amount of beer and the same dose of Antabuse as his fellow alcoholics who experienced the customary mild reaction. This was not only puzzling but was highly disconcerting since one had no way of knowing in advance which patient would experience the severe reaction.

Some years ago the mystery was solved, thanks to the work of a Swiss scientist named von Wartburg. He carried out an examination of the livers of people living both in the eastern and western worlds. He discovered that there was a deficit in a particular substance termed an enzyme in the livers of those living in the east, an anomaly which was quite uncommon among westerners. The existence of this enzyme deficit meant that those afflicted with it are short of a sub–stance necessary for the breakdown of alcohol in the body and, consequently, are unable to metabolise alcohol as efficiently as those who possess the enzyme in question. This explains why a Japanese may develop a flushing of the face after drinking a glass of whiskey, whereas this reaction would be unlikely in the case of an Irishman.

In more scientific terms, the absence of this enzyme means that the breakdown of alcohol in the body is arrested at the stage of acid aldehyde production. Acid aldehyde is an intermediate product of the combustion of alcohol in the body. The flushing of the face, palpitations, constriction of the chest, nausea and so on (i.e. the Antabuse reaction) is brought about by an excess of acid aldehyde. So too Antabuse inhibits the breakdown of alcohol in the body and produces an excess of acid aldehyde. Hence the excessive Antabuse reaction on the part of those individuals lacking the necessary enzyme and given Antabuse together with alcohol, as a test procedure.

Those for whom Antabuse is prescribed for the first time, often ask the question 'How safe is it?' This is a very reasonable query given the concern that exists today in respect of any form of medication. My response is that the taking of Antabuse, without alcohol of course, is less likely to produce side effects than would be the case with an aspirin. Obviously there is a small minority of people who are sensitive to Antabuse on its own, just as a few people cannot take penicillin. So too, in exceptional cases, certain individuals cannot touch a primula plant without breaking out in a rash.

How well does Antabuse work? Straightaway, I must point out that this is *not* a magic pill to cure any case of alcholism. In any event, there is no such thing as a cure for alcoholism. Combined with other forms of treatment, Antabuse can be a considerable help to many alcoholics anxious to give up alcohol. It can greatly assist them to place their feet firmly on the road to recovery. It is, however, a fundamental fact that, as with any other method of treating alcoholism, the efficacy of Antabuse will depend on the extent of the individual's will to get well. If the alcoholic has not the wish to recover from his alcoholism, much less the desire to give up alcohol as the first essential step to recovery, then Antabuse is not going to benefit him. There is no question of the

51

alcoholic swallowing down a tablet of Antabuse and thereby bringing about his instant recovery.

Advantages of Antabuse

The immediate practical advantages of Antabuse, broadly speaking, are twofold. In the first instance it will prevent impulsive drinking. If on a Monday morning the alcoholic suddenly experiences a feeling of frustration, boredom, annoyance or a sense of rejection — all common causes to rationalise the taking of a drink — then if he has already had his Antabuse medication he realises that he cannot drink alcohol until the following Saturday, by which time he will have taken measures to overcome the frustration, boredom, annoyance or sense of rejection.

The second advantage is perhaps even more significant. It may happen that some months after a course of treatment, out of a clear blue sky so to speak, when all is going well for the recovering alcoholic, he develops a sudden uncontrollable urge to drink. This can prove quite shattering. The alcoholic is now on the horns of a dilemma! He realises only too well just how important his sobriety is to him, and has already experienced some of its rewards. And yet the urge to drink may appear almost irresistible. His solution is to resort to the stratagem known as 'clock watching'. He decides, 'It is now nine o'clock in the morning and I will hang on until eleven, when I will have a cup of coffee and then see how I feel.' And for the next two hours, the minutes, even the seconds, seem to crawl by interminably. Come eleven o'clock, he takes the coffee and then postpones the decision until lunch-hour. And so throughout the day the alcoholic attempts to distract himself by going for a walk, toying with a book, etc. but his mind is dominated by the painfully slow passage of time as he keeps pushing back the moment of decision. Finally, the individual trapped in this situation may have the bright idea that with the bars closing at 11.00 pm he will go there at 10.45 on the grounds that he cannot do much damage in a quarter of an hour's drinking. He may or may not put this plan into operation. The point here, of course, is that the individual has spent a thoroughly miserable day tormented by indecision. Had he routinely taken an Antabuse tablet, he would have been spared all this anguish.

Arguments Against Antabuse

'What,' you might well ask, 'are the disadvantages of Antabuse?'

'Very few', is the answer.

Arguments advanced against the taking of Antabuse include, 'Doctor, I don't want to take Antabuse.' 'Why not?' 'Because my recovery won't be as good if I have to use a pill to get over my alcoholism.' Not so! Alcohol is a very crafty enemy for the alcoholic. All legitimate means to overcome this adversary should be employed. A recovery from alcoholism without the help of Antabuse is no more meritorious than one involving its use.

'Doctor, it is against the rules of the AA organisation to use Antabuse.' This is not the case.

'Doctor, I feel that if I take Antabuse, I will be using a crutch.' Well, what's wrong with using a crutch? Ask a man whose leg is broken. He is quite happy to use a crutch until such time as his leg has mended. Similarly, for the alcoholic a crutch can be very useful until he has recovered his confidence and is firmly set on the road to recovery.

'Doctor, I'm afraid to take Antabuse in case I accidentally took alcohol on top of it.' This is a possibility, but a remote one given that the user of the Antabuse should be aware of the highly unpleasant effects of an Antabuse reaction. In the event, the physician prescribing Antabuse should always inform the person for whom it is prescribed, of the nature of an Antabuse reaction and the consequences of it.

I recall an alcoholic refusing to take Antabuse on the grounds that if he were involved in a road traffic accident and rendered unconscious, some good Samaritan might come along and give him brandy in an attempt to revive him and by so doing provoke an Antabuse reaction which could kill him — and indeed, this might possibly be the outcome. However, this would be a highly unlikely combination of circumstances. Much more certain is the fact that the alcoholic who does not seek treatment runs a considerable risk of premature death from his abnormal drinking.

Mental Mechanisms

There are no aspects of the treatment of alcoholism where mental mechanisms are more commonly employed than is the case with Antabuse. These are simply ways in which the mind attempts to deal with some of the problems and difficulties of everyday living. They are quite commonly employed by all of us in the course of each day. People who suffer from problems brought about by their abuse of alcohol are particularly prone to use these mental mechanisms rather than face up to the unpalatable facts of their abnormal drinking.

DENIAL

Denial is the most basic of the mental mechanisms and is all too common a reaction on the part of alcoholics. Obviously, if an individual denies even the possibility that he may have a drink problem, there is no way he will be moved to face up to it. Denial is very often bound up with the term 'alcoholic' which is all too frequently used in a disparaging or negative fashion. As a consequence, victims of alcohol abuse are frightened off by this word 'alcoholic' and will take measures to ensure that their own drinking pattern is not brought under scrutiny.

I can appreciate this reaction only too well. I often see it in the case of some alcoholic patients who, after a week or two of exposure to a treatment programme, cannot yet accept their alcoholism. To these people and their families I would point out that the development of an alcoholic problem which necessitates treatment takes a considerable time, and cannot be put right in a matter of a week or two on a treatment programme. It is essential that the alcoholic should keep an open mind and, after reflection, in the light of the information they receive in the course of their treatment, they should discuss their reservations and misgivings in an open fashion with their therapists. As pointed out in Chapter 4, denial is bound up with a fundamental failure to accept the diagnosis and/or treatment.

RATIONALISATION

Rationalisation means the making of excuses to justify one's behaviour. This can be seen when the individual, confronted with a difficult task, rather than face up to it will take the afternoon off, go for a walk or perhaps play a game of golf, on the grounds that he will then be fresher and better able to deal with the matter. The alcoholic quickly becomes expert at rationalisation. Eventually, he reaches the stage when every day of the week he will produce rationalisations to justify his drinking. One striking example was brought home to me some years ago when an alcoholic patient was admitted for the fourth or fifth time, in a grossly intoxicated condition. After he was detoxified I attempted to ascertain from him the reason why he had relapsed. To my surprise he denied totally that he had taken drink. I then confronted him with the evidence of the nursing staff and the admitting doctor who had reported on his condition. When he persisted with his denial I asked him what had he been doing prior to admission. He replied that he had been out shooting and the weather had turned very cold. Consequently he drank some brandy from the flask which he always carried when shooting. He then stated that this could not be regarded as alcohol, since it was really medicine to prevent him developing the chest condition to which he was susceptible in cold weather. This, of course, was an extreme example of rationalisation. Minor versions are all too common in alcoholism, and all those people undergoing treatment of their disease would be well advised to look carefully at their own situation and ensure that they are not fooling themselves by indulging in rationalisations which can hinder their recovery.

PROJECTION

Another mental mechanism is projection. This involves ascribing to others our own faults or shortcomings. Again this mechanism is quite commonly employed by alcoholics. One sees it in the case of the individual with a serious alcohol problem, who blames his spouse for his own drinking and resists treatment on the specious grounds that the therapist's efforts should be directed to improving the behaviour of his wife. He sometimes contends that if his spouse would only treat him better he would have no problem with alcohol.

Consider too the case of the man admitted for treatment of alcohol dependency who, after a few days, becomes restless and insists on leaving against professional advice. Predictably, within a short space of time he suffers a relapse and now blames the treatment centre for this occurrence, claiming that he did not receive adequate treatment or consideration.

The use of the mental mechanisms by the alcoholic means that he continues to fool himself in respect of his drinking, rather than face up to the issue and seek help and treatment.

It seems to me that most of the arguments against the taking of Antabuse, carefully prescribed, are subtle forms of rationalisation. This was the view of a senior colleague of mine who helped a great many people to recover from their alcoholism. He frequently stated, quite bluntly, that if he came across an alcoholic for whom Antabuse was prescribed, and who refused to take it, then he was dealing with somebody who did not want to stop drinking. While this might appear to be an extreme view, I do believe, in the light of my own experience, that it is substantially true. It highlights yet again the necessity for an alcoholic to ensure that he is not making use of any of the mental mechanisms to the detriment of his recovery.

In essence then, if the alcoholic is to benefit from Antabuse, he must have a genuine wish to stop drinking as the first essential step to recovery. If this is absent then the alcoholic will find numerous ways to 'beat' the system, so to speak. He will resort to well-tried stratagems. He will switch the Antabuse tablet in the bottle and substitute unmarked aspirin. Or, after swallowing down a tablet of Antabuse, he will retire to the toilet, put his fingers down his throat and vomit it up. Sadly, the alcoholic who indulges in these manoeuvres is fooling only himself in the long run.

Positive Use of Antabuse

For Antabuse to be effective, the alcoholic taking it must regard it as a friend assisting him in his resolve not to drink. He must be positive in his view of Antabuse, and not regard the prescribing of it as an imposition which he has come to resent. He should at all times be aware that by taking it voluntarily after leaving the treatment centre, he is making an *affirmation* to himself that he is serious about his recovery. Moreover, he can regard it as an insurance against any sudden impulse to drink, and take comfort from the knowledge that even if he encounters unexpectedly a combination of circumstances which might put his sobriety at risk, he will not succumb. The taking of the Antabuse will also reassure those close to the alcoholic who are concerned about his recovery.

Administration of Antabuse

In practical terms, there are two rules which must be observed if Antabuse is to be used effectively. In the first instance the tablet should be taken only as prescribed. As I have pointed out, a small minority of people are liable to suffer a very serious reaction if they drink on top of Antabuse. A distracted wife may be tempted to conceal Antabuse in her husband's food out of desperation in an attempt to bring about sobriety. This of course is the abuse of Antabuse and should never be practised. Secondly, the individual for whom Antabuse is prescribed must make a decision as to how it should be administered. In this regard, I recall the mature recovered alcoholic who recently said to me, 'Doctor, I know it is irrational and silly of me, but if my wife so much as touches my bottle of Antabuse tablets, much less offers me one, I swear I will go off and take a drink. I am quite happy to take Antabuse myself and indeed find it of great assistance.' Conversely, I have been requested on many occasions by patients for whom I have prescribed Antabuse to ask their partners to give them the tablet each day as they cannot trust their memory where the taking of medication is concerned. Some recovering alcoholics are helped greatly by taking Antabuse under supervision, for example at an outpatient clinic or at a factory surgery in an EAP (Employee Assistance Programme) scheme, or at the surgery of their family doctor.

Antabuse should be taken each day, at the same time and in the same manner, so that it becomes as routine a procedure as brushing one's teeth or taking one's morning cup of tea.

For how long should Antabuse be taken? For as long as it is necessary. The basis for the successful use of Antabuse is that the decision to take it must be a *conjoint* one between patient and doctor. Equally, the decision to discontinue it must be taken *conjointly* by both these parties. Unfortunately if the patient stops it unilaterally this may often be the prelude to a relapse. Indeed some therapists hold that the discontinuing of Antabuse without the consent of the prescribing doctor is the first indication of an inevitable relapse.

Discussion

(a) *If the effects of Antabuse last for several days, why should it be taken on a daily basis?*
Firstly, because the voluntary ingestion of Antabuse is an *affirmation* on the part of the alcoholic that he is in earnest about his recovery, and a reminder to him of the necessity for sobriety. Moreover, human memory is fallible and the alcoholic taking Antabuse only twice weekly may suddenly realise that he has overlooked the last dose or two, and now finds himself contemplating a possible return to drinking with all the mental torment of the old drinking days suddenly revived.

(b) *If one has a relapse, how soon can one resume Antabuse?*
Twenty-four hours after the last drink.

(c) *Are there any foods or substances which should be avoided when taking Antabuse?*
Any food cooked in alcohol, such as chicken in a wine sauce, is safe. However, food served with uncooked alcohol, for example Christmas pudding and whiskey, must be avoided. Care should be exercised in the use of tonics containing large amounts of alcohol. Similarly, aftershave lotions applied too liberally might cause discomfort. If one is due to have an anaesthetic, the anaesthetist should always be informed that Antabuse is being taken.

(d) *What are the side effects of Antabuse?*
They can be divided into two groups. Those which are mild and general and might well be due to other causes: headache, stomach upset, fatigue. Then there are the rare but specific side effects such as peripheral neuritis, confusion, paranoid states. These side effects usually become apparent quite soon after the commencement of Antabuse therapy, which is why it is prescribed at the early stages of treatment, so that any side effects can be noted and corrective measures taken straightaway. On occasions, alcoholics taking Antabuse complain of drowsiness. This has led to some therapists advising that Antabuse be routinely taken at night-time.

(e) *Can Antabuse cause impotence?*
This is sometimes stated, but medical opinion differs as to whether it is so or not. Remember that alcoholism itself is a cause of impotence and indeed infertility.

(f) *If a patient had a severe physical or mental problem, would Antabuse be prescribed for such a person?*
In general terms the answer is no. However the art of good medicine is to consider each individual case on its own merits. An exception might be made if, after careful consideration, it was felt that the individual was well motivated towards recovery and anxious to take Antabuse as one of several measures to bring this about; then Antabuse or an alternative would probably be prescribed. The decision would be made having regard to the fact that if the alcoholic persisted in drinking, almost certainly he would kill himself, and in the process cause himself and all those close to him a great deal of misery and hardship.

(g) *If a person took Antabuse, could he be certain that he would never have a craving to drink?*
I could not say this would inevitably follow. However many recovering alcoholics taking Antabuse derive a bonus in terms of a freedom from craving for alcohol.

(h) *What is Abstem?*

Abstem is a substance similar to, but weaker than, Antabuse and commonly employed in the treatment of alcoholism. Broadly speaking, the facts outlined in respect of Antabuse apply equally to Abstem. It does not produce as severe a reaction as Antabuse if combined with drink, nor does it have the sometimes severe side-effects of Antabuse on its own which I have outlined. Furthermore, following a relapse it can be taken after a shorter interval than is the case with Antabuse.

(i) *What are Antabuse implants?*

These involve a minor surgical procedure when pellets of Antabuse are inserted under the skin. The theory is that Antabuse will be slowly and constantly released. This will ensure that when used in refractory cases of alcoholism, these individuals will be unable to drink.

In practice, this approach, which enjoyed a vogue some years ago, has not proved to be effective. Often the Antabuse pellet is extruded from underneath the skin, or produces an infection at the site of the implant. Moreover, the alcoholic lacking in motivation will often resort to drinking small amounts of alcohol on a continuous basis and over a period of time. By so doing, he will become immune to an Antabuse reaction and now proceed to drink excessively, out of resentment. He will rationalise his behaviour that he has had Antabuse forced on him.

For the well-motivated alcoholic, the cumbersome process of inserting Antabuse implants has no advantage over its oral administration when the alcoholic can affirm his determination to abstain, by the voluntary ingestion of Antabuse on a daily basis, rather than be teetotal for fear of suffering an Antabuse reaction.

7

Relapse

ALCOHOLISM CARRIES with it a high rate of relapse. This is a fact, however regrettable it may be, and one which must be acknowledged and confronted.

A relapse should always be treated in a positive manner and looked on as a learning experience. Indeed many recovered alcoholics with long years of sobriety behind them have attributed their ultimate recovery to the experience they gained, albeit painfully in some cases, as a result of slipping into a drinking pattern following their initial treatment.

Not for a moment would I contend that a relapse is either inevitable or desirable in terms of recovery. Many alcoholics proceed to make a successful recovery following exposure to just one course of treatment. Moreover, a relapse is always traumatic and occasionally hazardous and should be avoided if at all possible. If it does occur, however, the individual concerned should take advantage of the situation to learn from it by standing back and, in conjunction with his therapist, make an appraisal of all the circumstances connected with the relapse. As far as possible, the causative factors should be identified and a constructive plan formulated to deal with them in the future. This is yet another practical example of the application of the principle underpinning all worthwhile treatment programmes: the necessity for the alcoholic to take full responsibility for his recovery.

Realistic Expectations

That said, one must be realistic. On average it takes many years of heavy drinking to bring the alcoholic to the stage where sobriety is essential if he is to lead a healthy and a happy life. The cutting out of alcohol means a major change for the alcoholic and involves a great deal of adjustment. He must be given time to make this adjustment. It is important to reiterate that no alcoholic consciously sets out to develop the disease of alcoholism. If this fundamental fact is kept in mind, a much more realistic and reasonable view of alcoholism will result, bringing with it a greater understanding of the nature of the condition.

Unfortunately the entire field of alcoholism is bedevilled by a lack of understanding of many of the fundamental issues. For instance, as I have earlier emphasised, few people appreciate that alcohol for the alcoholic has an entirely different meaning than it has for the social drinker.

Another difficulty, this time for the alcoholic, is the indiscriminate use of the phrase 'the rewards of sobriety'. This has a seductive ring to it and can sometimes lead to unrealistic expectations on the part of the alcoholic, who may naively believe that he will straight away receive the recognition he believes he deserves for coping with his alcoholism. They forget that while the rewards of sobriety will 'appear' *in due course,* they take a varied length of time to manifest themselves, depending on individual circumstances.

On occasions alcoholics may become discouraged at what they perceive to be a lack of appreciation on the part of family or friends, of the very real efforts they are putting into their recovery programme. They may feel that there has been a diminution of interest, by contrast with all the attention which they received during their hospitalisation. They fail to appreciate that we live in a busy world where friends and families, however well disposed to the alcoholic, may be hard pressed to cope with their own lives. It is essential, therefore, that all alcoholics should keep firmly in mind the fundamental principle that they recover in the first instance for their own sake, no matter how devoted they may be to wife, husband, family or friends. Inevitably all of these parties will benefit from the well-being of the sober alcoholic who has achieved recovery by concentrating on recovering for his own sake.

Quite often I receive telephone calls from the families of alcoholic patients enquiring about their progress. On occasions, before I can respond to the query, I am exposed to a litany of recriminations against the alcoholic, together with a recital of all their shortcomings. This expression of hurt and frustration is only too understandable, but unless put to one side will do nothing to promote the recovery of the alcoholic, much less the welfare of the entire family. It is therefore essential for the families and friends of alcoholic patients to participate actively in a family programme. By so doing they will come to understand the nature of alcoholism as well as learning to deal with their own resentments and frustrations.

Before outlining the common causes of relapse, I would caution recovering alcoholics on the necessity for realistic targets. Recovering alcoholics sometimes try to do too much too quickly. However commendable their wish to make up for their shortcomings during their drinking years, they must remember that recovery will take time. I have sometimes seen alcoholics relapse because of frustration brought about by what they perceived as their failure to atone in a matter of weeks for the damage in the different areas of their lives, brought about by their abnormal drinking over a long period of years. Inscribed over the front door of St Patrick's Hospital, Dublin is the motto *Festina lente* — 'Hasten slowly'. This wise maxim should be borne in mind by every recovering alcoholic. Just as alcoholism itself is progressive, so too is recovery. The sober alcoholic, six months down the road to ultimate recovery, will be better able to cope with his life than was the case three months earlier.

Factors Which Lead to Relapse

ROLE IN FAMILY
The first one has to do with the change in the alcoholic's role in the family. Every family with an alcoholic member must make an adjustment to deal with this development. The adjustment may be good, bad or indifferent, but it is inevitable by virtue of the alcoholism of the family member concerned. However if after a course of treatment the alcoholic who is now 'dry' and starting on the road to recovery returns to a family where no readjustment is made in the

light of his change in status, tensions will develop, leading to frustrations which may precipitate a relapse.

Let me give an example to illustrate the point. The alcoholic housewife tends to be a solitary drinker and commonly funds her purchase of alcohol by 'fiddling' the household budget. When she is admitted for treatment, her husband perforce has to take on the management of the housekeeping budget. Obviously he will deal with this much more effectively and efficiently, but should he persist in continuing to look after the budget following his wife's return home from hospital she may well construe this as a vote of no confidence in herself. She may feel, 'I'm not being trusted. What's the point in persisting with the strenuous task of recovery?' This thinking may lead her to throw in the sponge and revert to drinking.

The important factor here is for partners and friends to accept that the recovering alcoholic must be treated differently, now that they have given proof of their intention to bring about their recovery.

JOB DIFFICULTIES

Job difficulties may cause relapse. Even today, one sometimes comes across instances where certain firms persist in carrying an alcoholic employee rather than confront him with his poor performance due to drink. It is only when the employee is taken off for treatment that positive action is taken. And so the employee may find himself, after a course of treatment, returning to a job where he has been demoted and his status diminished.

Fortunately, this situation is becoming increasingly less common for the very good reason that Irish industry, following the lead of the giant US corporations, is becoming much more enlightened in respect of alcoholism, and has come to appreciate that the recovered alcoholic becomes a trustworthy employee who contributes greatly to the activities of the company. Some years ago, the Electricity Supply Board pioneered an EAP (Employees Assistance Programme) in conjunction with St Patrick's Hospital, Dublin. So successful was it that many firms in Ireland have followed suit, and EAPs are now commonplace throughout industry in this country. In essence, they involve support and assistance for the alcoholic employee and family during his treatment, and a guarantee that the alcoholic's career will not be jeopardised, provided he makes a reasonable attempt to achieve recovery from his alcoholism. This means of course that the alcoholic employee must demonstrate a willingness to conform to an agreed treatment programme, with particular regard to the aftercare component.

RURAL LIVING

A difficulty applies to people living in rural areas where the opportunities for social life are more restricted than in the urban areas. And so the alcoholic, coming home after a course of treatment and feeling uneasy at the prospect of returning to his former drinking circle, may be at a loss for company since so much of social life revolves around the local public house or hotel bar. Indeed, in country districts there may be no other venues for socialisation. In this instance, a firm affiliation with AA will provide a ready-made solution to the problem of finding an acceptable social group, apart altogether from the other advantages resulting from active involvement in the fellowship.

There may be a further difficulty. It is now clearly established that alcoholics tend to drink in the company of heavy drinkers, some of whom may well have alcohol problems which they are not prepared to acknowledge. For these heavy drinkers, the return to the circle of the recovering alcoholic — now 'on the dry' and manifestly improved in so many ways — may be seen as a threat and prove too much for them to handle. As a consequence, tensions and strains may arise which will adversely affect the recovering alcoholic returning to his former drinking circle. It is essential therefore that the whole matter of their future social life be addressed by alcoholics during the course of their treatment, prior to their embarking on aftercare.

SENSITIVITY TO FANCIED SLIGHTS OR INSULTS

Fancied slights or insults may pose a real problem for some alcoholics following their return home. Many alcoholics are highly sensitive and believe that they are the subject of adverse comment as they walk down the streets of their home town: 'Look at Mike, he must have been very mad or bad to have been put away for treatment.'

It is essential that all alcoholic patients keep in the forefront of their minds the fundamental fact that *continuing sobriety is the answer to all criticism.* Do remember that few people are downright malicious, just as few people are entirely tactful in all circumstances. No alcoholic need be oversensitive to any criticism, real or imaginary, once they have given up alcohol. One major consequence of the increasing public understanding of alcoholism is the esteem in which the recovered alcoholic is now held, a development which would not have been thought possible 15 or 20 years ago. I come across this very often when I hear people speak in terms of admiration about recovered alcoholics some of whom, unknown to these people, had been patients of my own: 'Wasn't Mike great to have given up the drink when he was so heavy on it?'

Recovering alcoholics must steel themselves not to be over-sensitive, especially during the early days of recovery, and bear in mind, as I stated earlier, that *continuing sobriety is the answer to all criticism.*

OVER-SIMPLISTIC APPROACH

And then there is the *cut it out* approach to alcoholism which is so misleading. This involves an over-simplistic approach to the complex problem of alcoholism. 'Why all the talk about alcoholism? The simple answer is to cut out drink and get on with your life.' While the attainment of sobriety is undoubtedly the first essential requisite in recovery, there is much more involved. If this simplistic view were valid there would be no need for treatment facilities, for AA, Al-Anon and Alateen nor indeed for the very real concern commonly expressed at the failure or inability of many alcoholics to come to terms with their abnormal drinking.

OVER-CONFIDENCE

Over-confidence is the commonest cause of relapse. Let us take a practical example as to how this may manifest itself. An alcoholic comes for treatment feeling very poorly, with his morale at a low ebb because of the amount of alcohol he has consumed just prior to admission. He is straightaway detoxified and then exposed to the treatment programme. He feels much better and develops some measure of insight into his alcoholism. He is heartened by the support of family members who have affiliated with the family programme. By the time he is discharged, he has improved considerably. As a routine procedure he is counselled strongly to follow the aftercare programme. This he does for a time. And then, after a few months, he is assailed by doubts. 'Did the therapists appreciate the pressures I was under just before I was admitted?' 'The wife had been very difficult.' 'My health was at a low ebb.' 'I was subject to severe financial pressures.' 'Now, of course, my life is quite different.' 'My wife could not be more helpful or supportive.' 'My health is A1.' 'My finances are now back on such a sound footing that my bank manager lifts his hat every time he meets me.'

He fools himself that because his circumstances have improved, his alcohol problem has disappeared. And so he ceases to attend his weekly AA meetings, he cuts out his Antabuse and neglects his aftercare sessions. After a week or two free from Antabuse, very gingerly he may take a bottle of beer. Lo and behold, nothing catastrophic occurs! He does not explode. Nor does he turn green, white and gold or red, white and blue. And now he is certain that he is the victim of a huge confidence trick and so he presses on to take more alcohol. Often he appears to be controlling his drinking pattern until, sadly and inevitably, some crisis develops in an area of his life and now his drinking gets out of hand. Back he comes for another course of treatment, his relapse brought about by over-confidence and his failure to accept the maxim, 'Once an alcoholic always an alcoholic', no matter how much one's circumstances improve.

SELF-PITY
Self-pity may sometimes lead to relapse. This is quite under-standable since all of us are prone to self-pity from time to time. The alcoholic may well argue, 'Only 7% to 8% of all people who drink develop alcoholism. Why should I form

part of this small minority since I did not set out to become an alcoholic? It is not fair.' Of course it is not fair, nor indeed is life itself entirely fair to us at all times if we view it in these terms. Rather than brood destructively along these lines, the alcoholic should bear in mind that he is suffering from a disease, the relief from which can be readily brought about by his own efforts. The alcoholic should therefore take advantage of all the help that is available these days and get on with the task of recovery.

RESENTMENT

Resentment may sometimes bring about a relapse. Many alcoholics are deeply troubled by resentment brought about by a variety of causes, including a sense of outrage at having to be hospitalised. Furthermore, they may find it difficult to accept that they have developed alcoholism, while other members of their drinking circle — who sometimes drank more than they did — appear to have escaped the problem. This reaction may be so deep-seated and persistent that it will interfere with their recovery.

No alcoholic can afford to harbour resentment, which can be corrosive and destructive in the long term. Rather he should concentrate firmly on the positive benefits of recovery — the sense of liberation and the restoration to health and peace of mind.

LACK OF COMPASSION FOR ONESELF

A cause of relapse is failure to have compassion for oneself. Note that the term is 'compassion' and not 'pity'. Do bear in mind the fundamental fact that no alcoholic consciously sets out to develop the condition. This should help to counteract any tendency to negative brooding on one's misdemeanours. 'I must have a rotten streak in me to have drunk so much and behaved so badly.' This may well provoke another alcoholic to protest, 'No, you were not half as bad as me' and then proceed to catalogue a list of shortcomings so that a 'contest in depravity' now takes place. The problem here is that the alcoholic is giving expression to a strong masochistic urge born out of guilt for his or her alcoholism. This is quite negative and may lead to morbid ruminations which could well have disastrous consequences. Far better to think positively and get on with one's recovery, the best possible way to atone for one's shortcomings during one's drinking days.

SEDUCTION

Another cause is seduction. Here, consciously or unconsciously the spouse of the alcoholic will sometimes seduce the recovering alcoholic to resume drinking. This is not a common occurrence and is often difficult to identify.

At first sight it may appear incomprehensible that any wife or husband will want his or her spouse to drink again in view of all the misery of the past. However there are two reasons to account for it. In the first place, should the alcoholic stop drinking, the power which has been taken over by the other partner usually reverts to the recovering alcoholic. So accustomed has the spouse of the alcoholic become to wielding power within the family during the years in which the partner drank to excess, that he/she may be reluctant to forego it and will attempt to seduce the recovering alcoholic in differing ways to start drinking again.

In the second instance, the spouse of the alcoholic may derive abnormal emotional gratification from the sympathy and attention which they receive because of their partner's alcoholism. In simple terms they are 'getting their kicks' out of all this attention. The wife goes out for a walk, pushing the pram down the street and meets her friends and acquaintances. 'How are things, Mary?' 'Terrible. He's on it again. Last week the electricity was cut off. We can't pay for the groceries. Look at me, I haven't had a new coat in years.' 'Poor Mary.' And all down the street the story is repeated and the same response elicited.

DEPRESSION/ELATION

And finally may I draw attention to the connection between depression and/or elation and alcoholism. For many years past workers in the field of alcoholism have been only too well aware of this association (see Chapter 2).

Let me state emphatically that even if one has only the suspicion of depression or elation being a factor in one's history, one should look for professional advice and have an evaluation carried out. The treatment of manic depressive illness is highly effective these days and readily achieved by simple, straightforward measures. For those alcoholics prone to this illness, it is essential to have it properly treated. If not, apart from other unfortunate consequences, they run the grave risk of a relapse into their abnormal drinking.

Discussion

(a) *Does the term 'dry drunk' apply to somebody who has given up alcohol but has not come to terms with their having to do without alcohol?*

The term 'dry drunk' is often used to describe somebody who has given up alcohol but is full of resentment at not being able to drink anymore. I believe the reason for this unfortunate situation is inadequate treatment where the emotional and psychological problems of the alcoholic have not been identified and properly treated. The result is often an embittered individual with a chip on his shoulder, rather than somebody leading a normal life in every respect other than being able to take a drink, i.e. an alcoholic who has achieved recovery.

(b) *I often worry that I may fall into the trap of over-confidence. How can I avoid this?*

The fact that you are aware of this possibility is a healthy sign and a strong indication that you are not likely to 'fall into the trap', to use your own phrase. Moreover your attention to your aftercare programme means that you have not become complacent about your recovery. Regular observation of the aftercare programme will ensure that over-confidence does not develop with all its unfortunate consequences.

(c) *I suffer a great deal from depression. When I get depressed I feel the only solution is to take a drink, even though I know that I will pay dearly for so doing.*

I can sympathise readily with your predicament, so unpleasant are the symptoms of depression. However the modern treatment of depression is very effective and I would advise you strongly to seek psychiatric help. If you do so, I have no doubt but that you will feel better and be much happier in your life.

(d) *I have found that I tend to drink when things are going well, often after getting through a difficult time.*
This is not uncommon. It is sometimes called the 'New Year Syndrome' when alcoholics will steel themselves not to drink over the Christmas period, relax their defences and indeed sometimes rationalise that they have earned a drink because of their efforts to achieve abstinence over Christmas. This only strengthens the view that it is essential at all times to adhere closely to the aftercare programme.

(e) *I have worked hard to recover from my alcoholism and follow my aftercare programme conscientiously. My family will not trust me and keep me under constant surveillance, greatly to my annoyance.*
I can sympathise with your frustration. You must remember however that the confidence of family members has been eroded by repeated setbacks and broken promises over a long period. Consequently it will take time for trust to be re-established. Always keep uppermost in your mind the maxim that continuing sobriety is the answer to all criticism, as well as the basic fact that you work at recovery for *your own sake.*

(f) *In the early days of my recovery, I was frequently mortified and often tempted to relapse by friends and acquaintances who persisted in attempting to force drink on me.*
This happens all too often and is yet another example of the lack of understanding which still exists in respect of alcoholism. Many people are unaware that alcoholism can afflict anybody, and not just the unfortunate on skid row.

Prudence and good manners should dictate that individuals who refuse a drink would never be unduly pressed, or their abstention drawn to the attention of the company. This approach would make life easier for many recovering alcoholics, who however should always be prepared to be quite definite in their reply to offers of drinks, e.g. 'No thank you — I am off it on doctor's orders.'

Moreover, it should be borne in mind that according to some authorities, many teetotallers refrain from drinking as a defence against an unconscious predisposition to alcoholism.

8

Overall Treatment Plan

FOR THE GREAT majority of alcoholics, the usual picture is that of a transition from social drinking to heavy social drinking or alcohol abuse and then on to alcoholism. However this pattern does not prevail in every case. Some years ago we treated a young student just eight weeks after he had come to Dublin to study at the University. He had never taken a drink until he began to attend lectures at University and yet eight weeks later he was admitted with all the active symptoms of compulsive drinking. This story was so unusual that we looked into it very thoroughly and obtained several objective histories. At the end of our investigation we concluded that the facts as I have outlined them were indeed correct. The moral of the story is that each person suffering from an alcohol problem must be assessed and treated as an individual within a common framework of reference — a concept fundamental to all worthwhile treatment programmes.

An eminent doctor who was treated on several occasions before eventually making a splendid recovery from his alcoholism, always contended that alcoholism was a unique disease in the sense that recovery from it lay to a very considerable extent with the alcoholic himself, who had to assume the ultimate responsibility for his own recovery. To a much greater extent than is the case with practically any other disease, recovery is effected through the efforts of the alcoholic himself.

Some years ago the question of where the alcoholic should be treated was the subject of vigorous and sometimes acrimonious debate. Some held that the locale should be in a specialist centre treating only alcoholics; others claimed that alcoholics are best treated in a separate and discrete unit within a psychiatric hospital. Another view stated that the alcoholic was best placed in a general hospital, perhaps in a specialist unit. The reasons for and against all of these proposals were put forward with considerable heat by the protagonists concerned.

To my mind the debate is sterile inasmuch as no definite conclusion can be reached which will command universal acceptance. What can be stated definitively however is that the alcoholic must *always* be treated in a setting where a comprehensive programme is in operation. At all costs the pitfall of admitting an alcoholic to a general hospital or nursing home just to be dried out must be avoided. Such a procedure has been very properly dismissed as first aid, which will merely enable the alcoholic to become fit enough to commence drinking once more.

All proper treatment programmes of alcohol dependence must be ongoing and comprehensive. They must be ongoing in the sense that the alcoholic and his family are able to obtain help, support and advice over a considerable period of time. After all, if it takes many years of abnormal drinking — as is usually the case — for the alcoholic to reach the stage where alcohol is affecting his life so adversely that sobriety is the only alternative if recovery is to be achieved, this objective of total abstention will not be achieved overnight. Persistence and patience on the part of all concerned are essential.

An effective programme must be comprehensive. Alcoholism is a very pervasive disease, affecting all areas of the individual's life: physical and mental well-being, family relationships, social life and work. All of these areas must be examined and the appropriate corrective measures initiated. Anything less will at best produce a 'dry drunk', i.e. an individual who is not drinking but who is full of resentment and troubled by many unresolved problems. That is why the glib contention that alcohol is all that is wrong with the alcoholic is so misleading. Equally, one might claim that marriage is the cause of divorce.

A proper programme must incorporate the facilities and measures necessary to deal with the different areas of the alcoholic's life. This is a formidable task and one which can only be achieved by a multi-disciplinary team working in a unified way on the basis of an agreed philosophy. A practical model is one structured as follows. The alcohol team is led by a consultant psychiatrist with a special interest in alcoholism. Assisting him are highly trained professionals who are committed to the cause of helping alcoholic patients and their families. The team is comprised of psychiatrists, psychologists, counsellors, social workers, nurses and volunteers. They have available to them the services of a consultant physician who can call on other specialist medical colleagues when necessary. They work closely with the AA organisation as well as with Al-Anon and Alateen. Several meetings of these groups are held weekly in the treatment centre. The help of AA, Al-Anon and Alateen members is invaluable — all the more so because it is given so readily and selflessly.

This model is of course very often modified depending on the structure, staffing and approach of the individual treatment centre, for example the multi-disciplinary team need not necessarily be headed by a consultant psychiatrist.

Detoxification

Treatment is carried out in three stages. The first one is concerned with detoxification. This involves ridding the body of the poisons which have accumulated because of abnormal drinking. This part of the treatment occurs in isolation and often necessitates putting the individual to bed following a thorough physical and psychiatric examination. A carefully regulated short term dose of tranquillising drugs is now prescribed, together with large doses of vitamins in order to prevent withdrawal symptoms. At the same time the fluid balance is regulated. The general condition of the patient is constantly monitored. On average, and in uncomplicated cases, this process takes three to four days. The alcoholic is then allowed up and about and encouraged to affiliate with the next phase of treatment, that of rehabilitation.

Fortunately, these days, severe withdrawal states do not often occur, by contrast with the position some years ago when it was quite commonplace in a busy treatment centre to have several alcoholic patients gravely ill with DTs at any given time. Accordingly, detoxification can often be conducted on an out-patient basis. However if the individual is elderly, in poor physical condition or advanced in his alcoholism, successful detoxification may be a demanding process and dependent on the skills and on the medical and nursing care available in a properly equipped in-patient unit.

Rehabilitation

Once the patient is detoxified, treatment becomes a dual responsibility involving the therapeutic team together with the alcoholic patient and his family. So let us look firstly at the role of the therapeutic team at the stage of rehabilitation and aftercare, i.e. the second and third phases of treatment.

THE ROLE OF THE THERAPEUTIC TEAM

To my mind, the first duty of the therapeutic team is to ensure that the nature of alcoholism be explained to the alcoholic and his family. Every year large numbers of highly intelligent, well educated alcoholic patients are admitted to treatment centres. It never fails to surprise me how few of these people are aware of the basic facts concerning alcoholism and alcohol abuse, particularly when I consider all the exposure which alcohol abuse has received in the media over the past 20 years in this country. Obviously, knowledge of the basic facts of alcohol abuse and alcoholism is essential if the alcoholic is to take the responsibility for his recovery.

It has been my experience that exposure to a course of didactic lectures is the best basis for the dissemination of this information. These lectures should be constantly revised to incorporate all the worthwhile discoveries and new approaches in the field of alcoholism. They are of course combined with the reading of suitable literature, as well as being complemented by group discussions and one-to-one sessions between therapist and patient, together with attendance at AA meetings.

Group therapy for alcoholics in Ireland was initiated many years ago. As a routine, several different types of group therapy are conducted for the benefit of alcohol patients and their families. They include motivation groups, family groups and reality groups in each of which people with a common problem come together to discuss their reactions and feelings and to receive guidance on how to deal with their problems. Great benefit can be derived from these sessions when they are properly and professionally conducted. At all times the dignity of the alcoholic must be preserved, and care taken that while he is firmly confronted with the facts of his alcoholism, it is done in such a manner that no psychological wounds are inflicted which will continue to fester long after the termination of formal therapy. This principle is of course of great importance in the field of family relationships. It is the duty of the professional leading the team to ensure that it is observed in every case.

Individual counselling plays a large part in the programme. Here a close professional relationship is built up between therapist and alcoholic. An important benefit from this close relationship is that it helps to ensure aftercare is carried out on an ongoing basis for as long as is necessary.

In one treatment centre, hospital based, the nursing staff, who are in daily contact with the alcoholic are closely involved as members of the therapeutic team. So too are specially chosen volunteers: successfully recovered alcoholic patients who conduct an orientation group, where the matter of the alcoholic's adjustment as a sober citizen to life outside the hospital following his discharge, is dealt with in the light of the recovered alcoholic's own experience.

The therapeutic team must meet regularly each week when the progress of the individual alcohol patients is carefully reviewed. Measures necessary to deal with such complications as depression or family difficulties are discussed, decided upon and then implemented.

FAMILY MEMBERS

While relatives have always been involved in the treatment programme, in recent years there has been an emphasis on strengthening the family programme, in the light of increasing acceptance that alcoholism is so often a family problem — hence the active involvement of family members.

For one thing, none of us is totally objective where our own history is concerned, and so it is essential to obtain an independent account from a family member. Should this differ significantly from the version advanced by the alcoholic it is up to the therapist to decide where the truth lies. When such a conflict occurs, the experience of the therapist, combined with the passage of time, will usually elucidate the facts. Furthermore, it is necessary to assist the family members to come to terms with their own feelings, so troubled have they become in many instances as a result of the behaviour of the alcoholic family member. Moreover, relatives need guidance as to how best they can assist the alcoholic in his recovery (see Chapter 11).

SPIRITUAL HELP
Many alcoholic patients derive considerable comfort and assistance from spiritual help. The services of spiritual advisers with special knowledge of alcohol abuse, within the different religious denominations, are readily available. Over the years many alcoholic patients have commented spontaneously not only on the solace they have derived from their spiritual adviser, but also stressed the benefits that ensued in terms of their recovery.

USE OF ANTABUSE/ABSTEM
Antabuse or Abstem has been used for many years. Experience in treating alcoholic patients over the years has convinced me of the value of this form of therapy, properly used and taken in conjunction with other forms of treatment. Antabuse or Abstem can be particularly advantageous during the early months of recovery.

ALCOHOLICS ANONYMOUS
All alcoholic patients should affiliate with the AA programme, and their relatives with Al-Anon or Alateen. It is essential to attend a sufficient number of meetings to benefit from AA. Quite often I have heard alcoholics condemn AA for spurious reasons. 'Doctor, I could not stand the way the chairman kept a fixed smile on his face all through the proceedings', or equally trivial, 'Why did the chairperson wear such a silly hat which distracted me so badly?' Do give AA a fair chance and never lose sight of the fact that so many alcoholics have

been greatly helped by this organisation over the years. However, it must be stated that some alcoholics have a difficulty in accepting the AA programme and achieve recovery without recourse to the fellowship. So too, the approach of a particular therapist may not be advantageous in all cases, when some alcoholics may find the technique and personality of another therapist to be more beneficial.

LEAVE AND DISCHARGE

When to allow leave and when to discharge the alcoholic from the rehabilitation treatment is the responsibility of the director of the programme. It is essential to get the timing right. If leave is granted prematurely or discharge arranged before the patient is ready, the likelihood of recovery is diminished. These questions are therefore discussed in depth at the weekly team meetings when the wishes of the patients and their families are taken into account, in addition to the opinions of the team members as to the progress of the patient. We have learned that a graded system of leave, commencing with day leave and progressing to weekend leave works best in terms of ensuring the optimum time of discharge.

I am only too well aware of how heavily committed people are to their responsibilities in the different areas of their lives these days, and understand very well their concern to be discharged as soon as possible. That said, the priority for all alcoholic patients is to effect a recovery so that they will be enabled to lead healthy, happy lives without alcohol. For this goal to be achieved, it will be necessary to spend a certain length of time in treatment. The duration of stay will vary according to individual needs. That is why some alcoholic patients are discharged sooner than others. This can sometimes lead to misunderstanding and frustration. If the alcoholic undergoing treatment has any reservations on this matter he should make sure that he discusses them with his therapist who will be happy to explain the position, rather than harbour resentment against what they may perceive as unfair discrimination.

Finally the therapist must set up an aftercare programme for the alcoholic. In simple terms, the alcoholic who is most successful in achieving recovery is the one who is assiduous in following the aftercare programme. This fact has been proved conclusively by all worthwhile follow-up studies.

In practical terms, we recommend the three A's to alcoholics: Antabuse/Abstem for as long as is necessary, attendance indefinitely at AA, and affiliation with the treatment centre aftercare programme for as long as is recommended by their therapist. Regular reading of suitable literature is encouraged.

ROLE OF ALCOHOLIC AND FAMILY

Now to consider the measures to be taken by alcoholics and their families. In the first instance, the alcoholic must apply specifically to himself what he has learned in the course of treatment. This involves reflecting on the information on alcohol abuse and alcoholism with which he has been furnished. Coupled with this is the need for the alcoholic to indulge in constructive self-analysis based on this new knowledge when the positive and negative factors in his life can now be identified. These can then be discussed in detail with the therapists, and their relevance in terms of the alcoholic's recovery evaluated. At all times the temptation to indulge in a morbid re-creation of the past with resultant self-pity must be firmly resisted.

There must be a determination to get well and to effect a recovery from the progressive and crippling disease of alcoholism. This may be a surprising statement to some, given all the unfortunate consequences of alcoholism. But even in these days of economic pressures certain people are so well cushioned in terms of financial and family support that they are able to come for treatment, be detoxified and pay lip service to the programme before discharge, with no real intention of adhering to the aftercare recommendations. Inevitably they relapse and after a term of attempting to control their drinking, find themselves back in treatment once more.

What is wrong with this approach? It could be argued that if somebody wishes to start drinking again after a few months 'on the dry', and is prepared to take the consequences and bear the financial burden of a further course of treatment, that is his decision and right. The fallacy of this argument is that alcoholism is a progressive disease and the approach outlined above will inevitably lead to disaster, with some catastrophe (and I use the term advisedly) occurring, such as a car accident, overdose, a sharp deterioration in finances or the loss of the affection of someone near and dear. The message is very simple: there is only one time to deal positively with one's alcohol problem and that is *now*, before one has suffered needlessly and caused hardship and unhappiness to one's family and friends.

Remember too the ultimate fate of the victims of chronic alcohol abuse: namely repeated admission to hospital with eventual institutionalisation in the back wards of a psychiatric hospital, or perhaps permanent and irreversible brain damage, or jail. A study carried out on the population of the Irish prisons almost two decades ago confirmed the findings in other countries that many recidivists had serious alcohol problems. And the most sinister fact of all: premature death is all too common among chronic alcohol abusers.

The view has been expressed that initially the alcoholic should come to fear and dread what alcohol can do to him, and then proceed to learn to face everyday emotional upsets without resorting to alcohol. Only time will bring this about. That is why phrases such as 'the rewards of sobriety' which are so seductive, may be quite misleading. Fortunately for the recovered alcoholic, the rewards of sobriety will become a reality, but only after a time and *in due course* — three words which should always be borne in mind.

For the individual to accept all of the propositions which I have just outlined will necessitate the development of what one successfully recovered alcoholic used to call 'a state of mind'. In his view, the development of this state of mind was the sure proof of recovery. Some people are fortunate enough to arrive at this state of mind quite quickly, while for others it may take a lengthy period of time with exposure to several courses of treatment. However, once achieved, the alcoholic is now in no doubt that his life has taken on a new meaning. There is no longer a fear of alcohol, there is a rebirth of self-confidence and self-esteem, with a greater maturity which shows itself in the ability of the individual to deal successfully with the trials and tribulations which are part and parcel of everyday living.

There will be a rebirth of pride and ambition, not pride in the vulgar sense, but legitimate pride that one has successfully overcome the deadly disease of alcoholism. There should be a fresh ambition that one will lead a more satisfying life and in the process be a better husband/wife/ parent/family member/employer/ employee, and — let us not forget, in these selfish days — a better citizen. All of these aspirations are legitimate and are all attainable by the recovered alcoholic — *in due course.*

PLANS FOR FUTURE

For several reasons, the last week or ten days on the treatment programme are all-important. In the first instance, the individual concerned is usually feeling much better at this stage and able to apply his mind to the information received in respect of alcoholism and alcohol abuse. He will be more knowledgeable where family relationships are concerned and will have gained insight into himself and his emotional reactions. He will have reached the stage where he is now well equipped to make plans for the future in consultation with his therapist. In practical terms this will involve a consideration and appraisal of the different areas of his life.

In most instances, the alcoholic can count on returning to a family and job where support will be forthcoming. Should this not be so, then measures to deal with the situation must be decided upon. In all cases, the fundamental principle that the alcoholic recovers for his own sake must be kept firmly in mind. It may be necessary to modify one's lifestyle, for a time at any rate, after leaving hospital. This is very much an individual matter and one to be discussed with one's counsellor. It is essential to decide on a flexible plan to fill in the time formerly devoted to drinking. Practising alcoholics not only spend a great deal of time drinking, but also in plotting and scheming to ensure that they will be enabled to do so. The pursuit of sporting or cultural interests, the taking up of hobbies and involvement in charity work are all useful and satisfying ways of occupying the hours formerly taken up by drink. Regular attendance at AA, where one is in contact with people with similar problems, is very useful in this regard apart altogether from the other benefits deriving from affiliation with this organisation. In essence then, the last part of the treatment programme should be a time when the alcoholic is actively engaged in constructive plans for the future, in consultation with his therapist.

The development of physical fitness, apart from being desirable for its own sake, can give a welcome boost to morale and should be fitted into the treatment programme.

Above all, be assured that recovery is within the reach of all alcoholics with the exception of a tiny minority afflicted by irreversible brain damage. Alcoholism is a field bedevilled by 'doom and gloom'. We constantly hear of those people who relapse but seldom enough of the many who go on to recovery. The fact that there are so many recovered alcoholics enjoying and leading normal lives should encourage those starting on the road to recovery. While we cannot afford to be complacent, the success rate of modern alcoholism programmes are there for all to see, in terms of the many men and women who have been restored to health and happiness and enabled to achieve their potential, as a result of their compliance with these programmes.

Discussion

(a) *Can alcoholics return to normal drinking after a period of sobriety?*

This is the 64 thousand dollar question in alcoholism and one which has engendered much heated argument, culminating in legal proceedings in one instance in the USA. Let me state that in practical terms I do not believe anybody suffering from 'genuine alcoholism' in the sense of having had their disease definitively and positively diagnosed, can return to normal drinking. Such people may for a time indulge in a form of 'nibbling' with all sorts of restrictions built-in, which the ordinary social drinker does not have to bother about. It is essential in this regard that a long-term view be taken on alcoholism. Over the years, I have seen alcoholics, five, ten, fifteen years abstinent from alcohol, return for treatment after a period of 'controlled drinking'. In every case they admitted they were so ridden with guilt while drinking, and had to build so many restrictions around their drinking practices, that they derived little pleasure from it.

There is a further point, not sufficiently stressed, that life for the recovered alcoholic without alcohol is so satisfying they have no interest in returning to drink. To my mind this whole concept of controlled drinking by 'genuine alcoholics' should be set aside as it only does a disservice to the alcoholic, intent on achieving recovery, by diverting him from a commitment to the tried and proved notion of total sobriety as the basis for recovery.

(b) *Is total abstention necessary for alcohol abusers?*
No, but a modification of their drinking pattern is essential in view of the variety of social and medical problems resulting from alcohol abuse. Very often this can be achieved by brief counselling, simple advice and minimal intervention — strategies which are not adequate to benefit alcoholics, who require the comprehensive treatment set out.

(c) *How effective is the out-patient treatment of alcoholism?*
Treatment carried out exclusively on an out-patient basis is very effective in many cases so long as the principles of treatment which I have outlined are followed. These apply equally to all programmes whether exclusively out-patient or those incorporating an in-patient component as well as out-patient treatment. In many treatment centres, the duration of the programme is, on average, for 52 weeks with the alcoholic exposed to five or six weeks in-patient treatment, and the remaining 46 to 47 weeks given to out-patient care.

However, complicated cases are better treated initially in an in-patient setting, where the resources of the alcohol team can be readily deployed to deal with the different areas of the alcoholic's life which need urgent attention. Moreover, removal from his ordinary environment will help the alcoholic to concentrate on gaining the insight essential for recovery undisturbed by the distractions of his everyday life.

(d) *How would you decide that an alcoholic had recovered from his alcoholism?*
As soon as the alcoholic had achieved the goal of treatment, namely to lead a normal life as a teetotaller. Over the years I have found the all-important criterion is that the alcoholic should experience no sense of deprivation, having given up alcohol. This is readily apparent in the many alcoholics who have achieved a full recovery. They have come to terms with their abstinence and lead enjoyable and satisfying lives, by contrast with those individuals who have stopped drinking but are still resentful at not being able to drink.

(e) *I find that the regaining of my personal integrity is the chief benefit of my recovery.*
This I can well believe. For years, during their drinking days, alcoholics constantly compromised themselves by lying, until the telling of lies became so common that it eventually became an almost automatic response to any difficulty.

(f) *What are your views on the treatment of 'skid row' alcoholics?*
Unfortunately this small but seriously disadvantaged group of any alcoholic population is often overlooked. Essentially, this is a social problem even though the principle of the comprehensive approach to each alcoholic on an individual basis must always be observed. The provision of a network of hostels, half-way houses etc. is necessary if the needs of the 'skid row' alcoholic are to be met adequately.

(g) *How can I cope with the embarrassment of having to refuse an alcoholic drink while in the company of those with whom I formerly drank?*
By concentrating on the rewards of recovery. Remember too that the majority of people are not all that interested in the drinking practices of others, as long as they themselves can drink according to their own wishes. Moreover such drinks as Perrier water or the Irish bottled waters have now

the cachet of alcoholic drinks and are recognised as acceptable alternatives.

(h) *My work takes me out of the country quite often. How then can I follow the aftercare programme?*
AA is a worldwide organisation with many English-speaking groups. A large number of excellent publications on alcoholism in general, and on recovery in particular, are freely available and should be read on a daily basis. Some alcoholics find it helpful, especially in the early days of recovery, to keep in contact with their therapist by means of correspondence.

(i) *Is the treatment of alcohol abuse and alcoholism cost effective?*
The economic consequences of alcohol abuse and alcoholism are considerable, e.g. loss of production, increased health care costs. In the seventh Special Report to the US Congress on 'Alcohol and Health' from the Secretary of Health and Human Services (January 1990), it is clearly stated that alcohol treatment costs reduce general health care costs. Moreover, the popularity of the EAP over many years demonstrates their success in terms of improved industrial output. Some authorities favour out-patient treatment on the grounds of cost effectiveness. I believe that a balance must be maintained (see (c)) if alcoholics are to receive the most appropriate and effective treatment. In general terms, the better the treatment the more cost effective it will prove.

9

Prevention

'ALCOHOL IS a substance which is used wisely and well by the majority of people who drink, and who derive nothing but pleasure and benefit from its use. Alcohol is also a drug which can miserably wreck or destroy life, and which exacts these costs on a devastating scale.' These are the opening sentences of a special report prepared by the Royal College of Psychiatrists as far back as 1979. The problem posed in developing an approach to alcohol in our society which will help to prevent alcohol abuse while not interfering with the legitimate use of alcohol by social drinkers, is as difficult today as it was twelve years ago. It is essential to strike a balance and avoid the over-reaction so often provoked by the subject of alcohol. Relying solely on such measures as hefty price increases or punitive laws is neither effective nor prudent. Rather the emphasis should *first* be placed on informing the public on the dangers of alcohol abuse and the need for responsible drinking.

Quite frequently the statement is made by recovering alcoholics that had they been aware, at the start of their drinking careers, of the basic facts concerning alcohol and alcohol abuse, they would not have indulged in the excessive drinking which brought about their alcoholism. They deplore the fact that they never received any worthwhile information on the subject either during their schooldays or subsequently. In many cases, they now have the laudable ambition to share with their friends and family the knowledge of alcohol and alcoholism newly acquired in the course of their treatment. By so doing, they hope to prevent others from making the same mistakes that they have made. This view must be appraised in light of the widespread and constant coverage which alcoholism has received in the media in the past 15 to 20 years.

There is certainly grave concern over the prevalence of alcohol problems, not just here in Ireland but throughout the western world. A great deal of misery is suffered by individuals as a result of alcohol abuse, and devastation brought about at family, community and industrial level. This has led to a demand that resources should be made available to promote the concept of prevention, and vigorous measures necessary to bring this about be implemented. Indeed the economic argument that it is cheaper to prevent alcoholism than to treat it is one which commands considerable support. Unfortunately this is sometimes pushed too far, for example, when it is postulated that alcoholism is not a disease but a self-inflicted condition resulting from excessive indulgence, or at the very least, induced by a faulty lifestyle. This assertion demonstrates not merely a failure to understand the nature of alcoholism, but a lack of compassion for its victims, none of whom consciously sets out to develop the disease.

The matter of prevention is a highly complex one which can be approached at many levels and in a variety of ways. I shall attempt to outline some of the more important issues relevant to it. For the sake of clarity I propose to deal with it under two headings: (a) formal measures and (b) informal measures. I would emphasise however that these two approaches are interlinked and should take place concurrently.

Formal Measures

LAWS AND REGULATIONS
Formal measures involve laws and regulations. If these are invoked wisely and command the support of the citizens, they can be highly effective. To be successful they must be in accord with the traditions and values of the society concerned. In Denmark, for instance, statutory measures in this area are less harsh than is the case in Sweden, where a more authoritarian approach to excessive drinking has been in force for some years.

In the USSR, so concerned had the authorities become over the increase in alcohol abuse in that country that they brought in far-ranging and restrictive legislation in 1985, which included measures to reduce the production of alcoholic beverages, the limitation of the sale of alcohol and a crack-down on the home distillation of *samogon,* the Russian equivalent of moonshine or poitin. These measures were rigorously enforced. It now appears however, that the pro-gramme has run into serious difficulties in spite of some early successes, notably in the reduction of road accidents, absenteeism and the death rate. Some commentators claim that the reason for this setback was the zealous manner in which the law was enforced, before the population in general had been persuaded of the necessity for changing their atti-tude to drink and modifying their drinking practices.

PRICE

Since 1960, real income has doubled while the price of alcohol has increased by 20%. Therefore, in relative terms, alcohol is now cheaper than it was 30 years ago. This fact was highlighted a decade ago by the Edinburgh-based psychiatrist, Professor Robert Kendell, in a paper entitled 'Alcoholism — A Political and not a Medical Problem' which generated considerable interest and discussion. Kendell pro-posed that scarce resources are best spent on prevention, and went on to argue that raising the price of alcohol would lead to a reduction in consumption and a consequent diminution in alcohol problems. This was in line with the Lederman theory which postulated that a reduction in per capita consumption of alcohol in a population brought about a decrease in alcohol problems. In my view, this approach is a blunderbuss one which illustrates yet again the danger of producing simplistic solutions for complex problems. Far better to follow the recommendations of the Irish National Council on Alcoholism (INCA) that the government should adopt a pricing policy for alcoholic beverages which would ensure a reasonably constant relationship between the price of alcohol and the amount of disposable income. It also urged that alcoholic beverages be removed from the cost of living index, so that a rise in the price of alcohol would not bring about a demand for a wage increase to compensate for the rise in the index resulting from the new, higher price for alcohol — the vicious circle syndrome. That said, the price of alcohol should not be allowed to fall again. However, the entire question of pricing and alcohol will be affected to a considerable extent within the next few years by EEC Regulations designed to produce fiscal harmonisation in this area within the member states.

AVAILABILITY

This is a difficult subject because it has been shown that different sections of the community tend to over-drink in different social situations; for example, social group 1 has the highest expenditure on alcohol, as well as drinking proportionately more wine and less beer. Limiting the availability of alcohol to the general population does not always result in a decrease in overall consumption, as demonstrated by recent experience in the USSR where the production of samogon has soared.

Nevertheless, when we look at the drinking scene in Ireland, certain measures to curb availability come to mind straightaway. High on the list is the question of exemptions and extensions. There has been a five to six-fold increase in the numbers granted over the last number of years. At the very least, a more selective approach to the granting of these extensions and exemptions is a matter of urgency.

SALES TO YOUNG PEOPLE

The raising of the minimum drinking age to 21 years, as is the practice in most states within the USA, commands considerable support. For this to be effective, identity cards giving proof of age would need to be introduced. Some years ago this measure was considered at government level but rejected on the grounds that it would not be practical to enforce it at that time. However, there is also an authoritative view that it would be more practical to retain the present legal age of 18 and concentrate on vigorous education campaigns directed specifically at young people who might well be more readily persuaded to defer drinking until age 18, rather than 21. Meanwhile, of immediate importance is the necessity to enforce the present legal age. In addition the entire question of the sale of off-licence liquor needs re-appraisal.

As a practical measure, the employment of young people in lounges, bars, etc. should be discontinued.

ADVERTISING

There is in existence in this country a code designed to curb the advertising of alcohol on television and radio. Following the introduction of this code, the advertising of spirits has been banned from television and radio. The same restrictions do not apply however in the case of the print media.

Indeed it is by no means as certain as people might believe that restrictions on the advertising of alcohol will necessarily bring about a major decrease in consumption. This was a conclusion arrived at some years ago at an EEC seminar on the subject in Luxembourg. At a recent conference in London, under the auspices of Anglo-Irish Encounter, advertising industry representatives argued forcefully that expenditure by different drinks groups for advertising purposes was aimed at brand promotion within a static market. It is essential however that agreed guidelines in respect of drink advertising be strictly observed. Only careful and continuing monitoring will ensure that this is achieved.

DRINKING AND DRIVING

The penalties for drunken driving must always be rigorously enforced. Here in Ireland, many people hold that the present limit of 100 mgs is too high and should be reduced. In the first consensus statement to be agreed by representatives of all the Medical Royal Colleges in the UK and Ireland at the end of 1987, among other proposals to deal with alcohol abuse at community level, the recommendation was made that because a large number of drunk driving offences occur among inexperienced drivers, a first step should be to lower the permitted level of blood alcohol for drivers for the first two years after passing their driving test. The consensus statement then went on to advocate the introduction of highly visible random breath testing.

91

It is important to remember that alcoholics are very prone to be involved in road traffic accidents and offences. In a paper published in 1973, Professor Anthony Clare and myself showed that a random sample of 100 hospitalised alcoholic males were responsible for 163 accidents, as against 66 for the 80 controls studied, with a preponderance of serious accidents in the alcoholic group. At the time, we recommended that all those drivers found guilty of drunk driving be examined to ascertain if they were suffering from alcoholism. If this were the case, then treatment should be made available on the lines of 'constructive coercion' so that the risk of further involvement in road traffic accidents by these alcoholic drivers — so often the case, as our study showed — would be minimised. This recommendation was supported in essence by the Whitaker Commission on Penal Reform which reported in 1985.

Here I must pay tribute to the late District Justice Michael McGrath, who pioneered a Court programme in the Midlands almost twenty years ago. He ordered drivers convicted of driving offences to undergo a programme of education in respect of alcohol abuse and, by so doing, succeeded in starting many hitherto undiagnosed alcoholics on the road to recovery.

Informal Measures

Before putting down the details of these measures, may I reiterate that prevention should always be viewed as a package where formal and informal measures are complementary and both approaches are used simultaneously.

Essentially, informal measures are aimed at bringing about a change in public attitudes to alcohol, alcohol abuse and alcoholism. During the 23 years of its existence, INCA played a major role in this area. The Health Education Bureau was also involved. It published a considerable amount of literature as well as providing an educational pack for use in schools. Its functions and those of INCA have now been taken up by the Health Promotion Unit of the Department of Health which is assisted in this task by the Health Advisory Council.

Some years ago I delivered a lecture to a group of teachers in the West of Ireland. In the course of it I stated that education was the key to creating a public awareness of the problem of alcohol abuse and was essential for the adoption of sensible and safe drinking practices. At the end of the lecture I was challenged politely but firmly by one of the senior teachers present who informed me that he, as a teacher, was tired of being told that education was the answer to all of the problems that beset our society, from alcoholism to unemployment. He made the point that this was too facile a view and placed too much of an onus on teachers who were commonly perceived as having sole responsibility for education.

His point was well taken. It is all too easy to leave education on alcohol to others. All of us, the citizens of this country, have a duty to inform ourselves accurately on the facts concerning alcohol and alcohol abuse so that we are now not merely in a position to disseminate these facts to others, but are also prepared to apply them to our own drinking practices. Never forget that an ounce of example is worth a ton of words, a point particularly relevant in a country where verbosity rather than eloquence is often the order of the day!

The Government through its agencies has of course a responsibility to ensure that clear, factual information on alcohol and alcohol abuse is freely available to the public. *How* this is best achieved is by no means clear and requires further research. Educational campaigns must take into account such considerations as our ambivalent attitude to heavy drinking, the existence of the many myths and fallacies in this area and the differing abilities of sections of the community to comprehend the message because of discrepancies in levels of education and intelligence.

Media campaigns at national level while helpful, are not necessarily the answer in themselves — apart altogether from their high cost. They should be combined with more specific approaches at local level and aimed not only at the general public but at selected groups such as school-goers, professional, sporting, commercial and social organisations.

Considerable care must be taken to ensure that the information is presented in a balanced and acceptable form so that charges of bigotry and fanaticism cannot be levelled at the presenters. The approach most likely to make an impact on the section of the community being targeted should be carefully considered, since it has been clearly demonstrated that within the context of providing information on health matters to the public at large, the use of specialised techniques geared to different sub-groups is imperative.

INFORMATION

The type of information to be disseminated was spelled out in practical terms some years ago by the Royal College of Psychiatrists in its publication *Alcohol and Alcoholism*. It recommended specifically: (1) that the public should be informed that alcohol is a drug; (2) that it be stressed the use of alcohol to relieve unpleasant feelings when bored, frustrated, etc. is dangerous; (3) that there should be public disapproval of intoxication — as far as this country is concerned we should endeavour to reverse the image of 'the hard man'; (4) that people who dispense hospitality should have regard for the welfare of their guests. They pointed out moreover that anybody who takes a drink must assume personal responsibility for his actions as a result. Driving a motor car was a good example of the point made. Indeed it is encouraging to note that many people nowadays make arrangements for independent transport home if they go out to a social function which will involve drinking. I feel strongly that in this country many drinking practices such as the round system which, I am glad to say, shows evidence of dying out, and perhaps more pernicious, that of 'forcing drinks' on people, could well be criticised under this heading.

A further recommendation stated that clear indication should be given as to what constitutes a safe level of drinking. This recommendation has been significantly revised in a recent update by the College. It now states that up to 21 units of alcohol per week for men, and 14 units per week for women, represent safe limits of drinking. It also makes the point that it is unwise to make a habit of drinking consistently at these levels. In practical terms a unit of alcohol is

94

defined as a half pint of beer, a glass of wine or a small measure of spirits. This change in the upper limit of safe drinking is highly significant. It demonstrates a new consciousness that alcohol, when consumed consistently at levels formerly considered safe, can adversely affect the health of the individual. It has become much more widely appreciated that medical and surgical wards of general hospitals contain a striking number of patients whose illness has largely been brought about by the unwise use of alcohol.

It cannot be stressed sufficiently that one does not have to conform to the popular image of the advanced alcoholic to suffer grievously from the effects of heavy drinking.

RECOGNISING THE WARNING SIGNS

So too while many people may be aware of the classical signs and symptoms of alcohol addiction described in earlier chapters, there is not the same appreciation of warning or prodromal signs frequently displayed by alcohol abusers. These include: (1) absenteeism, particularly of the Monday morning variety. Studies in Ireland have confirmed the findings of other countries, that heavy drinking is the commonest cause of this type of absenteeism from work, and indeed is a significant reason for absenteeism in general. (2) A tendency to meet with an unusual number of minor accidents. For obvious reasons, alcohol abusers are notoriously prone to meet with accidents resulting in minor fractures, sprains, cuts, abrasions, etc. (3) Hypochondriasis. Many heavy drinkers worry a great deal about their health. They constantly consult doctors and fail to disclose to them their drinking history. They are sent for numerous blood tests and X-rays and no significant findings result, as a rule. As soon as they stop drinking their symptoms disappear, and they now experience a level of well-being that they would never have believed possible during their drinking days. (4) Problems with children. School failure, emotional disturbance and delinquent behaviour are often attributable to the alcohol abuse of one or both parents. (5) Out-of-character behaviour for no apparent reason. Aggression, either physical or verbal, and based on mild paranoid reactions induced by excessive drinking, is not uncommon at a certain stage of alcohol abuse. (6) Material deprivation. If one enters a home where the material conditions are not nearly as good as the income going into this house would suggest, one should suspect the existence of an alcohol problem.

Experience has shown that there is no simple answer to the problem of prevention. We should however take heart from the recent experience in the USA, where a much more balanced approach to drinking has become the order of the day. This is reflected in the diminished demand for spirits. Overall, it now appears that Americans are drinking less. An encouraging feature of the alcohol scene in the US is the greater understanding of people suffering from alcohol problems, brought about, as I see it, by such factors as the success of the EAP programmes, and the readiness of well-known personalities to acknowledge in public the existence of their own alcohol problems and their success in achieving recovery through their exposure to treatment programmes.

Discussion

(a) *Do you think soft drinks are too dear and that there are not enough of them available?*
Yes, I do. I believe soft drinks are over-priced and we have not enough variety. Many recovered alcoholics complain to me about their difficulty in finding a palatable soft drink.

(b) *Should the promotion of 'non-alcoholic' wines and beers with a minimum amount of alcohol be encouraged?*
Yes, and indeed there appears to be a growing market for them.

(c) *Do you think the medical profession is doing enough in the field of alcohol abuse, particularly family doctors?*
This is a criticism which I have heard made on many occasions. I believe the position has improved considerably in recent years. I am highly impressed by the knowledge of alcoholism displayed by many family doctors who are very understanding of the difficulties of their alcoholic patients and go to considerable lengths to assist them. However

to my mind there is a need for more enlightenment at consultant rather than family doctor level, given the large number of alcoholic patients in the wards of general hospitals. Still more emphasis in the medical undergraduate and post-graduate education programmes on the subject of alcoholism is necessary.

(d) *The opening hours of public houses in Scotland have been extended and an improvement in the drinking habits in that country is purported to have resulted. Why can't we do the same here?*

The results of this fairly recent move in one region of Scotland have certainly been encouraging so far. Whether this approach would work as well here in Ireland is, at the very least, questionable. There is evidence from other countries, notably Finland where they abolished restrictions on the opening hours of licensed premises, that this can lead to an increase in alcohol consumption and heavy drinking.

(e) *Why doesn't the government do more to prevent the development of alcoholism?*

The government is doing a great deal in the area of prevention and has done so in the past. The preparation of a national policy on alcohol is well advanced. I believe however that any government can only do so much. The rest is up to individuals to exercise their democratic right to drink responsibly within the generous limits of the current licensing laws.

(f) *Do you think there is too much drink supplied at official functions as well as at commercial ones?*

I do, in general terms. While I believe that hospitality must always be generous, I think it is regrettable that we have reached the stage where it is considered necessary to offer what I believe to be an excess of alcohol at all sorts of receptions, openings, etc. This has the effect of tempting people to drink far more than they might otherwise do. It seems to be overlooked that it is not *appropriate* to supply only alcohol on these occasions when an attractive variety of soft drinks should also be provided, as well as tea and coffee.

(g) *Do we, as a nation, drink far more than other countries?*

This is not the case. Figures show that on the table of per capita consumption of alcohol in the EC, we are quite low down the list. But it has to be stressed that approximately 20% of the drinking population consumes almost half the alcohol drunk, according to some authorities. This fact reinforces the point that it is all important to promote the concept of responsible drinking, so that this minority of drinkers will not find themselves so vulnerable where alcohol problems are concerned.

Another heartening development of recent times is the adoption by the drinks industry of a much more helpful attitude towards alcohol abuse and their advocacy of the concept of responsible drinking.

(h) *Can the Government afford to put a very high tax on alcohol in view of the loss of revenue which would follow decreased consumption?*

The problem posed by this question illustrates yet again the need for balance when changes in the price of alcohol are to be considered. Excessive drinking, determined to a significant extent by relatively low price and consequent high consumption, costs the state a great deal because of medical treatment and decreased industrial productivity — an effect to be measured against the revenue produced by a high consumption rate, as well as the employment of many people throughout the drinks industry, from production to marketing and sales.

10

Women and Young People

PERHAPS THE most striking changes in the Irish drinking scene have to do with the increase in alcohol consumption on the part of women and young people. This is in line with the European experience as highlighted in the WHO publication 'Targets for Health for All'.

Women

In accord with custom, let us consider women and alcohol first. Sadly, statistics show that for some years past the number of women being treated for alcohol dependence has risen substantially to the point where they now constitute one-quarter of all admissions for alcoholism. This represents a significant change from the situation which prevailed some time ago, when women alcoholics were outnumbered nine to one by men. That said, let me emphasise that far fewer women than men develop alcoholism, although they have all the same reasons to do so, with some additional ones thrown in for good measure.

Today there is general acceptance of women drinking in public. This has been brought about by a number of factors. Women's rights are now widely recognised. A large number of women continue working after marriage and have the money to fund their drinking without being dependent on their husbands for it. Career women are better paid and have more income at their disposal to spend as they see fit. The advertising industry recognises these facts and increasingly aims its campaigns at women. The traditional Irish pub, where only men drank in semi-darkness, is long gone, and has been replaced by modern lounge bars attractively fitted out to attract the two sexes and commonly with food and entertainment laid on.

However the increased tolerance for women taking a social drink does not extend to those women who develop problems with alcohol. There is much less sympathy in our society for women alcoholics than for men who develop the disease. Unfortunately this shows itself all too frequently in the lack of support on the part of husbands. Time and again this becomes apparent in alcohol treatment programmes when, in my view, many women alcoholics are unfairly disadvantaged by having to virtually 'go it alone'.

As to actual consumption, it must be remembered that women's bodies are of smaller volume and contain more fat than do those of men. Consequently in similar circumstances women cannot handle an equivalent amount of alcohol. Moreover recent research findings suggest that there is a qualitative difference in the way that the bodies of women deal with alcohol. That is why the upper limit for safe drinking is put down at 14 units per week for women, while 21 units are recommended for men. Failure to recognise this difference sometimes results in young women attempting to match drink for drink with their boyfriends — with disastrous results. Cirrhosis of the liver is more common in women than in men, again a pointer to the necessity for extra care by women in respect of their drinking practices.

SPECIAL FACTORS

Among the factors particular to women with drink problems is firstly an ambivalence towards their new role in society. While women welcome their relatively new-found freedom, the obligations and responsibilities brought about by it may create a conflict which sometimes leads to emotional upset. In turn, this may cause the women concerned to turn to drink for relief. This is sometimes the case also with mothers who often have to bear a disproportionate share of the trauma brought about by problems with their children. And then there is the plight of the lonely and neglected housewife who seeks solace in drink. In her young days she may become frustrated by being cooped up in suburbia, burdened by the responsibility of child-minding without adequate help, and missing the company of her work-mates which she enjoyed prior to marriage.

In middle age, the same sense of isolation and loneliness may be present now that the children have left the home, with the problem aggravated by the change of life, occasionally complicated by depression. In both instances, the women concerned may be aggrieved at what they perceive as a rejection or certainly a lack of support by their husbands who spend most of the time out of the house, either at work or enjoying social life with their men friends. Solitary drinking may result through regular and furtive purchases of alcohol in the supermarket. It never fails to surprise me that this type of drinking behaviour can often go undetected for long periods in spite of the out-of-character behaviour which results. This is demonstrated by such significant signs as unpredictable moods, neglect of duties and responsibilities, an undue preoccupation with physical health, irritability and constant complaints regarding family finances which are of course being regularly eroded by the necessity to fund the secret drinking.

FOETAL ALCOHOLIC SYNDROME

Some years ago it was discovered that children born to a sample of women alcoholics who drank during pregnancy suffered gross physical deformities resulting in a number of similar defects, most notably a distinctive facial appearance together with a sub-average level of intelligence. A follow-up study carried out ten years later on these same children demonstrated that not only did these defects persist, but additional physical complications were now apparent including hearing and visual problems. The condition was labelled the 'Foetal Alcoholic Syndrome'.

This study has since stimulated considerable research into the effects on infants of prenatal alcohol exposure. It now appears that the prevalence of the Foetal Alcoholic Syndrome is in the order of one to three per 1,000 live births. This rate however varies according to location and the population under study. From these findings it follows that only a small percentage of women who drink alcoholically during pregnancy give birth to babies with the Foetal Alcoholic

101

Syndrome. We are now informed that the most significant contributory factors to prenatal alcohol damage include persistent drinking during pregnancy by women with chronic alcohol problems, a previous history of alcohol problems in the mother, large families, and race.

Another highly significant finding by researchers engaged in this field, and a disturbing one, is that while the Foetal Alcoholic Syndrome is linked to maternal alcoholic drinking during pregnancy, more moderate levels of maternal alcohol consumption sometimes produce adverse effects much less obvious and not so easily identified in the offspring.

Much more work remains to be done in this field before we have a complete understanding of the effect of maternal drinking on offspring. As an instance, the role of socio-cultural factors needs to be elucidated much more precisely. Nevertheless at this moment two conclusions are apparent: (1) We do not know the safe limits of alcohol consumption for pregnant women. (2) Accordingly, prudence would dictate that all pregnant women would be well advised to refrain from drinking.

Young People

For some years, a growing concern has been expressed over the abuse of alcohol by young people in this country. Their tendency in some cases to drink overtly and excessively on the announcement of Intermediate and Leaving Certificate examination results is causing widespread disquiet. That said, it is important to remember that only a proportion of young people indulge in anti-social behaviour because of drink, or indeed suffer mental or physical damage through alcohol. Nevertheless representative bodies as disparate as parent groups, officers of the law and organisations within the drink trade, have come to echo the opinion put forward by professionals including psychiatrists and social workers, that there are increasing numbers of young people in the country who tend to abuse alcohol. Support for this view is afforded by statistics which show that the first admissions to psychiatric hospitals for the treatment of alcoholism in persons under the age of 25 years has increased considerably.

There are many reasons to account for the present position. Adolescence is a time of transition characterised by self-doubt and uncertainty. One might argue that these difficulties have been accentuated in this querulous age by the constant questioning of previously held standards and values. More often than not, no positive or acceptable answers are forthcoming, resulting in uncertainty and fears frequently suppressed rather than articulated.

The pressures within the schools brought about by the emphasis on academic achievement are a source of considerable distress to the youth of today and are often compounded by the projection of parental anxiety in this area. The spectre of unemployment is there to haunt our school-leavers, constantly exposed to dire predictions of a shortage of jobs for the foreseeable future. Lack of occupation leading to a way of life lacking purpose and personal satisfaction is a grave consequence of youth unemployment.

For the young people of today, drinking is not just viewed as socially acceptable but almost as a necessity if they are to conform to the values of their peer group. It has not only acquired a legitimacy but has been invested with a glamour that is all too seductive. The pub has become the usual meeting place for young people, the centre of social life: for some, the only outlet.

Contributory causes

Other social and cultural factors have combined to bring about the present position. The large increase in alcohol consumption over the past 20–30 years in Ireland is a reflection of the prominent part alcohol now plays in so many areas of Irish life. Inevitably, the increase in drinking by parents has influenced the attitude of their children towards the role of alcohol in their own lives. Paradoxically, at a time of high unemployment, the increased spending power of today's youth has enabled them to fund their drinking on a scale which would have been impossible some years ago. The relative affluence of many young people today and their willingness to spend a greater part of their income has made them the target for intensive advertising campaigns.

So vigorous had these become in respect of alcohol promotion that an acceptable code for the television and radio advertising of alcohol was drawn up some years ago. This code is subject to constant review, but does not apply to drink advertising in the print media.

EFFECTS OF ALCOHOL

As I have earlier pointed out, all forms of intoxicating liquor, sold legitimately, contain a substance, ethyl alcohol, which has addictive properties. Moreover alcohol is a depressant drug — a fact often overlooked, particularly by young people because of its immediate effect in reducing inhibitions and acting as a 'social lubricant'. Small wonder then that it has been termed the 'domesticated drug'. It is also a potentially toxic substance, capable of causing physical and mental ill effects when abused, apart from the more obvious social damage. The spectre of 'lager louts' rampaging at football matches is all too visible.

Fortunately only a minority of those who drink become dependent on alcohol and develop the condition of alcoholism. The modern view as outlined in Chapter 2 is that many factors contribute to bring this about: drinking habits, occupation, personality traits and heredity being among the more important. Of major significance is the level of tolerance for alcohol abuse within the community of which the drinker is a member. The effect of the different factors and their relative importance varies from person to person. The importance of peer pressure is particularly significant in the drinking practices of young people.

Given the widespread acceptance of drinking as part of their normal lifestyle, the temptation to seek relief from the pressures, tensions and anxieties in their lives is a very real one for young people today. The fact that one should be physiologically and psychologically mature to handle the drug, ethyl alcohol, is often disregarded. So, too, is an awareness of the properties of alcohol and its effect on one's body and level of intellectual functioning. The existence of alcohol related disorders, the causation of alcoholism, its nature, and — most pertinently — the manner of its earlier manifestations, are all matters which receive little if any attention from the young drinker.

In some cases, young people who develop alcohol related problems have a history of emotional upset or may be socially disadvantaged. Those youngsters who are the products of unstable homes, with resulting emotional deprivation, are highly vulnerable where alcohol is concerned. Moreover numerous studies have demonstrated that the children of alcoholic parents are more at risk of developing the parental problem. The abuse of alcohol leading to acute alcoholic poisoning can be viewed as a cry for help, if not as an actual attempt at suicide, phenomena which have become more common in recent years in this age group.

Alcohol abuse in the young can present in a variety of ways, and those dealing with them should be on the alert to this fact. Anti-social behaviour which can on occasions bring the individual into contact with the law, is often precipitated by excessive drinking. Such behaviour may be aggravated by concurrent abuse of other substances, perhaps leading to cross addiction. Academic under-achievement and poor attendance at school may be due to alcohol. So too may a deterioration in the health, both physical and mental, of the youngster drinking to excess. Difficulties in interpersonal relationships, both within and without the family circle, are sometimes directly attributable to alcohol abuse. The association between sub-average performance at work and absenteeism — notably of the Monday morning variety — and alcohol abuse, must always be kept in mind.

CLINICAL SIGNS

Clinical signs of alcohol dependence may become manifest in young people who regularly drink more than is good for them. These include blackouts (i.e. memory loss), gulping drinks, consistent lack of control over the amount consumed, and aggression, verbal or physical. Bout drinking and the development of withdrawal symptoms are always of sinister significance.

PARENTAL EXAMPLE

Let me stress here that the importance of parental example cannot be over-estimated. These days more than ever before, young people will not tolerate admonition in respect of their drinking habits from adults whose own drinking practices are at variance with their advice.

EDUCATION

As with all forms of education, an integrated approach between home and school should be observed. Care should be taken to ensure that there is not a conflict between the advice given at home to young people in respect of alcohol and that offered in the school. Education on alcohol must be presented in a balanced fashion as part of an overall approach to health. A welcome development is the recent launch of two new Alcohol Education Resource packs for young people. These are DAY (Drink Awareness for Youth) and a video, 'Handle with Care', produced by the combined efforts of the Health Promotion Unit of the Department of Health and the National Youth Council of Ireland in the case of DAY, and those of Veritas Video Productions in association with the Health Promotion Unit in respect of 'Handle with Care'. DAY is designed to assist youth leaders integrate an alcohol programme with other educational activities for young people, while the video and teachers' guide 'Handle with Care' is aimed at children in the 10–15 year old group. Another worthwhile development in this area is the production of Irish-made films on alcohol abuse and alcoholism to enable Irish youngsters, as well as the general population, to identify more readily with the issues raised by them, than would be likely in the case of many foreign films with their differences of culture and idiom.

TREATMENT

Young people who develop alcohol dependence should be exposed to properly mounted alcohol programmes in accordance with the principles set out in Chapter 8. Emphasis must be placed both on the positive goal of recovery and on the consequent rewards in terms of maturity, personal satisfaction and better functioning as the fundamental aims of treatment, rather than the negative one of mere abstention from alcohol.

In Ireland, we are fortunate to live in a society where the individual is free to exercise his right to drink within the generous limits of the licensing laws. Sadly, in many instances this right is not exercised with a proper degree of responsibility. To my mind, a radical reappraisal of our national attitudes towards drinking habits and the abuse of alcohol is urgently needed. Until this comes about, and a healthy respect for alcohol based on the recognition of its potentially harmful effects if abused becomes firmly established in the minds of all, our young people in particular continue to be at risk. If they are to achieve a satisfying way of life, it is necessary for these young people to learn the responsible use of alcohol and to be aware of the hazards of alcohol abuse. They will then be in a position to make a decision as to whether they wish to drink or not, rather than feel themselves forced to do so, which is substantially the case at the present time when the right *not* to take a drink seems to be eroded to a substantial extent.

Only through proper health education promoted within the family, and reinforced and extended in the schools, can this objective be attained. This is a formidable challenge, and one which needs the wholehearted support of all of us through practice as well as precept.

Discussion

(a) **Should women alcoholics be treated on their own special programmes and separate from men?**
This approach has been advocated. One can argue for and against it. I believe that a compromise where women have special activities within the overall programme common to both men and women, is perhaps the most practical procedure to follow.

(b) **Would you agree that emotional factors seem to be more important in bringing about alcoholism in women than is the case with men?**
Yes, I would. I am regularly impressed by the response I receive from women alcoholics when I question them on their views as to why they develop a drink problem. Nearly

always they will advance an emotional reason, often bound up with some difficulty in a relationship with their husband, boyfriend or children. I don't believe that this is necessarily the sole cause of their alcoholism which is of course a multi-factorial disease. But the notable point here is that women are quite definite in their own minds about their emotional difficulties, by contrast with men who tend to produce more general answers covering a wide variety of reasons to account for their alcohol dependence.

(c) *What, in your view, is the single most important measure to be taken to improve matters in respect of alcohol abuse by young people?*
Undoubtedly, example on the part of adults in contact with youngsters, i.e. youth leaders, game coaches, teachers, and — most important of all — parents. This is an area where an ounce of example is worth a ton of talk. Then when the good example of moderate drinking is apparent, the concerned adult is in a position to counsel the youngster in a positive way not to rely on drink for relief, but rather to look for a more satisfactory way of dealing with the problems which are part and parcel of adolescence.

(d) *One often gets annoyed with the fact that youngsters seem to spend so much time in public houses. When challenged, they say they have nowhere else to go to meet their friends.*
I share your concern. Young people claim that there is nowhere else to socialise with their peers other than pubs where, incidentally, underage drinking is often tolerated. Certainly there seems to be a shortage of coffee shops where formerly young people were able to meet and socialise. However do not forget that throughout this country there is a wide spread of activities with excellent facilities in the different areas, notably sport and the arts, where young people can meet up and enjoy themselves if they so wish. But first of all they must get away from the notion that all leisure activities begin and end with drink. This will involve a massive reappraisal of the role of alcohol not just in respect of our young people but in all our lives.

(e) **What are the 'No Name Clubs'?**

These were started in Kilkenny in 1978. They are social clubs for teenagers where no alcohol is served. They are now located throughout the country and have a very useful function.

11

A Family Illness

ALCOHOLISM IS a progressive illness with a high morbidity and mortality rate. It is also a family disease. The illness affects each and every member of the family and active help is required to diminish its impact. Unlike many other conditions, alcoholism embroils family members in its development and consequently these members are deeply affected by its manifestations. In the throes of the disease, the drinking itself is often the only distinguishable symptom that separates the alcoholic from his family. This accounts for the often quoted comment, 'For every alcoholic there are three or four dry ones.' As with the alcoholic himself, family members are caught up on an emotional roller-coaster which may lead to severe emotional trauma and loss of self-esteem.

Why is it called a family illness? Mainly because of the severe emotional effects but also because alcoholism tends to run in families. There is much debate in this area. Some experts believe that it is due predominantly to hereditary factors, others to environmental ones. The truth is that it embraces both. And so people with strong family histories of alcoholism, particularly in the first and second generations, need to exercise that bit more care in the consumption of alcohol. Families need also to be more communicative about a history of alcohol abuse. I believe that many unnecessary problems have occurred as a result of the reticence in this area in the past. A significant number of alcoholics have parents or grandparents themselves treated for alcoholism at some stage. Some of these have grown up believing that the reason that 'Dad drank too much' was because mother did not understand him properly, i.e. 'she nagged him too much'. They have heard this from him over and over again, and the belief has been further confirmed by their mother's silence, i.e. her attempts to shield the children from the truth. In general, with regard to alcohol abuse, children need to have the facts sensitively explained to them at the earliest stage possible. This will help them to make informed choices in relation to alcohol consumption later on.

'If only he knew what his drinking really does to us he would stop.' Family members, neighbours, employers and health personnel spend a lot of time pleading to alcoholics to stop for their health's sake, their children's sake, their job's sake or their life's sake. They threaten the alcoholic that if he does not stop he will lose his health/children/job/life. Their tones are supportive, aggressive, punitive or pleading. They do not understand the plain fact: that the alcoholic will not stop for someone else's sake. He will only stop when he arrives at full acceptance of the condition and develops real motivation for self-change. This acceptance comes from the profound realisation of the extent to which alcohol has disrupted his life.

It is not profitable to attempt to plead with alcoholics to stop drinking, much less to set out to batter the alcoholic into a reaction of guilt in the spurious hope that this will 'make' him stop. It is however important to help the alcoholic to appreciate the damage that alcohol has done to himself by looking at its effects on the family.

The field of alcoholism is full of paradox: for example to gain victory you have to accept defeat; to regain pride you need humility; and in order to make amends to the family you must first make amends to yourself. The same is true for family members. Much time-wasting energy is spent trying to change someone else, but all one can reasonably do is to work on changing oneself as well as creating circumstances or 'space' for the other person to change. In my experience, recovery is often instigated by family members who discover this reality and make adjustments to their own situations. As an instance, a key issue is responsibility. Very often, in alcoholic homes during 'wet' or drinking phases, too much responsibility is taken by the spouse and/or the children, while too little responsibility is assumed by the alcoholic. When the family accept responsibility only for their *own* behaviour, the alcoholic may realise he needs treatment and start on the road to recovery.

Effects on the Family

No two people are the same, no two alcoholics are the same, no two families are the same; so it is very difficult to attempt to describe definitively the unhappiness created by alcoholism in the home. One is reminded of Tolstoy's famous dictum, 'All happy families resemble each other, but each unhappy family is unhappy in its own way.' The range and scale of difficulties experienced by families of alcoholics are vast. It is tempting to discuss only what appear to be the most extreme instances, cases of severe physical and sexual violence or of gross neglect. These are of course extremely damaging and can lead to lifelong resentments and severe difficulties. However broken promises, a missed commitment or an inappropriate conversation, the everyday emotional consequences in a drinking alcoholic's home, are also traumatic. Sadly, sometimes drunken alcoholics disclose to their children information that they should not hear, burdening them with severe dilemmas of conscience at far too early an age. For example one teenage girl told me that her father, while drinking, disclosed to her an affair he had had, but begged her not to tell her mother. The problems for the family are many and varied: debt, neglect, violence, inconsistency, fear and death. Fear is probably the most universal consequence, not just a fear of violence, but fear of the future and fear of the unknown. The alcoholic can readily identify with these fears — illustrating yet again the family illness concept of alcoholism.

Let me give another case illustration. The wife of an alcoholic, a man in public life who used to drink after-hours, told me of the terror that gripped her when her husband returned in a drunken state in the early hours of the morning. This did not happen every night, but the problem for her was compounded by the fact that she did not know on which night it would happen again. At this stage he was not particularly violent in the physical sense, although this had been the case in the past. He would however demand a meal as soon as he staggered in. He would stand at the cooker and bash it with a saucepan until his wife came down from the bedroom to prepare a meal. Sometimes she would try to resist, but inevitably this involved wakening the children and the neighbours because of the row that ensued. As the years went by, he only had to beat the cooker once for her to spring to attention 'for peace sake' she said, but at a huge price for her nervous state in general and her self-esteem in particular. This story illustrates the psychological intimidation and helplessness which can occur, and the lengths to which family members will go to obtain peace, even if only short-term and at a heavy price.

Much work has gone into describing the development of alcoholism from a family perspective. The different stages are best described as follows.

Stage one

Typically, at the first sign that there is a problem with alcohol, family members complain and ask that the drinking be not repeated. They are usually met by defensiveness, and may now regret having raised the topic. They are therefore more reluctant to bring up the subject again. As the illness develops they are told by their extended family or by well-meaning outsiders that the way to solve the problem is to change their own behaviour. This is the start of the process in which family members take responsibility for the problem by blaming themselves. The alcoholic also rationalises his behaviour by criticising the family. So typically the spouse will attempt to become a better cook/provider/lover/ housekeeper/more interesting/less introverted/more outgoing/ more glamorous and so on, in an effort to remove the causes of the drinking, never realising that these causes lie elsewhere.

Once the illness is established it becomes impossible to deny it, and the family now turns its attention to getting rid of it. Shame and guilt are the order of the day, so that the family becomes more and more isolated socially as it tries to solve its own problems and avoid social contacts to conceal the truth. They believe that the core fact is they have failed to stop one of their members from drinking excessively, and that this represents a reflection on themselves. This reaction may be compounded by the stigma of alcoholism, as they see it. Accordingly, attempts to cover up the problem increase as more and more traumatic drink-related instances occur.

Another difficulty is that the problems present inconsistently and intermittently. In 'dry spells' the alcoholic will attempt to compensate for bad behaviour, for example by lavishing the family with gifts and promises. And now the family may even question the existence of a serious problem. For all of the family, this Jekyll and Hyde behaviour is very difficult to cope with, but particularly so for younger children who crave consistency. Threats become more commonplace but are seldom carried out. 'If you take one more drink I will leave.' 'The next time you come home drunk, I will not be here.' 'I will tell my teacher what you said.' And so on. The family become obsessed with alcohol and spend most of the time wondering what things will be like 'when I get home', 'when she comes back'. 'What will happen at the wedding next month?' 'What will I do if my friends find out?' 'How will I cope if he loses his job?' 'Will the kids be damaged?' etc. The children are often used as 'pawns' or as 'go-betweens'. Sometimes one child is singled out for special treatment from the alcoholic, while another will be made into a scapegoat, perhaps because the former goes along with the drinking while the latter does not. Or sometimes it just happens because of the capricious thinking of the drinking alcoholic.

STAGE TWO

At this stage, the family usually have no long-term goals and so become 'enablers' or co-alcoholics. The enabler may also be a colleague, employer, neighbour or health professional. An enabler is anyone who unwittingly supports or encourages the alcoholic's drinking. For example one 16-year-old daughter of a female alcoholic told me that she would buy alcohol for her mother because her mother would then sleep and stop being abusive. One husband told me that he had drunk with his alcoholic wife in the false hope that this would prevent her from overdoing it. A brother of an alcoholic arranged for a drunk driving charge to be squashed in a futile attempt to help his brother stop drinking. Many family members spend wasted hours pouring alcohol down sinks, and ringing publicans to ask them not to serve 'their alcoholic'. One man told me that he had spent much time in his teenage years touring the local pubs at night in order to drag his alcoholic father home. The point here is that all attempts to control the alcoholic's drinking are doomed to failure if the alcoholic does not accept his condition or does not have the motivation to stop. 'Enablers' succeed only in taking responsibility away from the alcoholic and in placing an excessive burden on their own shoulders.

STAGE THREE

As all attempts to control the drinking fail, the situation for the family deteriorates into the third stage, 'disorganisation', and a 'what's the use?' attitude is adopted. Short term peace is still the priority and often the alcoholic is considered a management problem rather than a person. This is known as the 'elephant in the corner syndrome'. If one can imagine having a large elephant in the sittingroom — never mind how it got there — the problem is to keep it happy so that it does not cause havoc. All its needs are met but still the problem is too big to contain! There can now develop considerable violence — emotional, mental, physical and sexual. It must be remembered however that the perpetrator may be the non-alcoholic spouse or other family member. One lady told me that she kicked her husband as he lay drunk, following his objectionable behaviour. Such events cause great guilt and shame. Sexual difficulties are commonplace. It is not surprising that the non-alcoholic spouse finds love-making distasteful with a drunken spouse. If he is rejected continuously the alcoholic may come to believe that the spouse is involved with someone else, or will taunt the partner causing severe distress and, in some instances, sexual difficulties that last well into recovery.

STAGE FOUR

Sooner or later a crisis will occur. Family members can precipitate such a crisis by withdrawing their support for their loved one's drinking. The non-alcoholic partner usually assumes every role in the household at this stage. Following a crash or a medical emergency or job difficulties, the alcoholic will seek help and go on to recovery. Or perhaps he will relapse and fall back into a more disappointing phase, all the worse because the family's great hope of 'treatment' has been dashed. Of course recovery can still be achieved at a later stage.

STAGE FIVE

The next phases are bound up with the family's attempts to escape from the problem and to manage their lives without the presence of the alcoholic. In this situation the children may leave home or leave the country to escape from the trauma, or the spouse may leave temporarily or permanently. In all cases however the emotional stress for the family continues even when the alcoholic is no longer on the scene. This is understandable in view of the huge emotional investment from the family prior to the separation, and their concern for the safety and well-being of the alcoholic. They sometimes feel guilty and are deeply concerned that the wrong decision may have been taken. This situation could be likened to a grief reaction, and is one with which it takes a long time to come to terms. It has to be noted also that marital separation is still not universally accepted in the Irish context.

Children of Alcoholics

In a family with an alcoholic member actively drinking, the children struggle to make sense of the situation and battle to survive. Different children adopt different coping roles. Some may act out or behave badly in an attempt to gain attention or to turn the family focus away from the drinking. Some will become 'entertainers' for all the family, operating in a frivolous vein, never taking things too seriously on the surface at least in order to offer light relief for the family. Some will withdraw into themselves and thus attempt to ensure minimum problems for the family. Some will become over-achievers in an attempt to gain self-esteem and recognition from outside the family circle.

In living with a drinking alcoholic, no child survives without emotional trauma. Many experience severe abuse and neglect and suffer emotional scars that they will bear well into adult life. I have often heard alcoholics in the early days of treatment make comments such as 'my drinking has never hurt my children', or 'they have always got what they wanted'. Sadly these comments are misinformed and display an ignorance of the awareness and needs of children. Within my own experience, children of alcoholics have attempted suicide, missed school, under-achieved, over-achieved, experienced learning and behaviour disorders, opted out and have used and abused alcohol and drugs as a direct response to parental alcoholism. The child who experiences physical and/or sexual violence is of course at extreme risk of developing physical, emotional and mental health problems which may persist.

ACOA

An organisation called Adult Children of Alcoholics has grown up in the US and spread to this part of the world. Although the long-term effects on children are only now being properly researched, the presence of such an organisation and the massive attendance at their meetings does signify the existence of long-standing problems for the children of alcoholics. One of the problems which adult children of alcoholics seem to experience is a difficulty in forming and keeping trusting relationships. Family members of alcoholic households at all stages report feelings of embarrassment and shame brought about by parental alcoholism. The biggest single consequence however is that the drinking alcoholic deprives his children of himself. This applies to all children of alcoholics. In the absence of recovery, children simply never get to know their drinking parent or appreciate what they are really like. Unfortunately, relationships with the non-alcoholic parent are also strained because of the general tension within the home. Where both parents are alcoholics, the problems for the children are, of course, much more severe. Generally speaking, the earlier that recovery is effected, the less serious the consequences for the children.

Many of the children presenting with a variety of symptoms to the child psychiatric services are there as a result of alcoholism within the family system.

Spouses of Alcoholics

For many years I have been involved with a spouses' group on a weekly basis. This group is made up of the nearest relative of both in-patients and out-patients. Ninety per cent of these are spouses, hence the title of the group. The group is open-ended and the length of participation is at the discretion of each member following discussion with his therapist. Some attend for only one or two meetings, most for a minimum of ten sessions, and some attend regularly for up to three years. It is a great advantage to have experienced members in the group as they demonstrate its efficacy by their obvious recovery. Their presence is an active encouragement to new members. There are usually two or three new members in the group each week. They come to it nervous and apprehensive, unsure of the purpose of the group. The rest of the group helps these individuals to adjust by their obvious support and concern for them.

Alcoholics are often reluctant to 'allow' or encourage their spouses to attend the group meeting in the belief that this might be a haranguing session, where all their personal difficulties are discussed in public. In fact spouses are actively discouraged from talking about the alcoholic partner and are asked to focus on their own strengths and weaknesses. As one man put it, 'I went along with the sole purpose of getting my wife sober. At that stage I felt I was in full control of the situation. However as time went on I was to learn that I was there for myself. I came to appreciate that as my attitude changed perhaps my wife might seek help for herself.' Some spouses resent going, 'It is my husband that is sick, I do not need to change.' An important function of this group is to enable members to see themselves as people in their own right, and not just the 'wife of' or the 'son of'. On occasions therefore, when introducing himself, the spouse is asked to talk about his first name and how he feels about it, thus promoting his sense of his own identity.

Time is allowed for people to dwell on their own hopes, strengths, weaknesses and achievements. Often group members ask each other about the positive measures they undertook for themselves in the intervening week. The sharing of feelings and experiences is a considerable comfort. While anger and fear are probably the most difficult feelings to report, an atmosphere where *all* feelings can be reported is created by the willingness of the group to do just that. Many fear that they will be disloyal if they talk about their problems, but often this reluctance to talk or the wish to remain private perpetuates their problems by keeping them hidden. Sharing feelings of resentment and bitterness is encouraged, but lengthy repetitive accounts of instances where they were victimised are discouraged, as this can lead to self-pity and stultify personal growth.

A considerable part of group time is devoted to the concept of responsibility. Initially members are inclined to blame themselves for their partner's drinking. It is a relief for the spouse to realise that he did not cause the alcoholic to drink to excess. As a member learned, 'One thing will always remain uppermost in my mind, and that is, no matter what I did or said, I could not prevent my wife from drinking if she so decided.' This seemingly simple concept of accepting responsibility only for one's *own* behaviour is difficult to grasp for people who have been 'over-responsible' for years, and living with people who have been 'under-responsible'. New balances must be established. One member of the group wrote 24 full pages concerning all the consequences of her husband's drinking. Later, following discussion at the group, she admitted that at least half of what she had written was not in fact due to her husband's behaviour, but rather to her own inactivity and shortcomings. His drinking was a convenient 'dumping ground' for all the problems. Release from such pressure liberates the spouse and starts the healing process.

Coping styles used by spouses vary greatly. Most aspire to the Al-Anon philosophy of 'emotional detachment' from the problem of the person. As mentioned earlier, some are not only spouses of alcoholics but may be sons and daughters of alcoholics. This sometimes leads to soul-searching: 'Is it something in my personality that made me choose an alcoholic as a partner?' or, 'Is it something that I have done that caused the drinking?' Many writers have also addressed this issue. Whalen believes that there are four personality types of wives of alcoholics: 'Wavering Winifred', 'Suffering Susan', 'Punitive Polly', 'Controlling Catherine' — thus implying that these women marry in an attempt to satisfy conscious or unconscious emotional and personality needs (Thelma Whalen, *The Quarterly Journal of Studies on Alcohol 1953–14, 632*). Of course this theory is sexist and does not take account of the fact that spouses will adopt all four roles and many more besides at different stages and in response to the problem.

Alcoholism can obscure many other difficulties within a family. In a small number of cases, the marriage may not survive following sobriety because of fundamental marital conflicts covered up by the drinking. In all cases the presence of marital strain can never be properly assessed however without a lengthy period of sobriety. Having been through so much trauma during the drinking sessions it is not surprising that many spouses have difficulty coping with their partner's sobriety. This may be a time of great uncertainty. There is often considerable resistance to making positive changes in the spouse's own lifestyle. Such resistance can be explained by a reluctance to change which results from the fear of a recurrence of the problem and the habit-forming one-up/one-down nature of the relationships where alcoholism exists. Family relationships must be expertly and sensitively handled if further guilt and self-blame are to be avoided. Group members often discover needs within their own personality which contribute to difficulties within the relationship. For example one lady realised that she was able to satisfy a 'caretaking' role within herself while her husband was drinking, a need which she had developed as a child because her own father was an alcoholic.

Many questions of a practical nature are discussed at the spouses' group: 'Should I keep drink in the house?', 'Should I bring up the past?' and queries such as 'What if she drinks again?' Predictably, the impact of alcoholism on children receives much attention.

Socio-Cultural Considerations

Cultural attitudes that shape behaviour in this field must be considered. Sadly there is still a wide acceptance in our society of excessive drinking, particularly on the part of male drinkers. The reasons for this are complex and have their roots in our historical past. Misplaced tolerance is all-important in the context of the family. Although socio-cultural attitudes are changing, it is probably true to say that the Irish wife and mother is given and takes too much responsibility for her male counterpart. It is very common to hear the shortcomings of the male alcoholic being ascribed to the failure of his wife to take care of him properly! Some women in the spouses' group complain that when they married they immediately became mothers to their husbands and feel trapped in that role. As a nation we seem to accept our lot in a fatalistic way, as evidenced by the often-used phrase 'It could be worse!' This is probably an important reason why unacceptable behaviour is not seen as such. In the course of therapy, the exploration of some of these socio-cultural considerations and discussions on sex roles by the alcoholic and family members can be very beneficial.

Treatment of the Family

The modern view of alcoholism treatment in general is that it should be geared to the specific needs of the individual. Thus in some cases reality therapy will be vital, while in others one-to-one counselling may produce a better result. In the majority of cases a combination of different forms of treatment, where appropriate, is best. So the matching of treatment to individuals is crucial. During treatment family members may require one-to-one counselling because their self-esteem and confidence have been eroded. They must always be encouraged to persist with treatment on their own account. In a small number of cases referrals to other services are necessary, for example for the severely depressed spouse or for the profoundly disturbed child. Support groups such as the spouses' group, Al-Anon (for the adult family members) and Alateen (for the teenage children of alcoholics) should always be invoked. Marital counselling and family therapy are also used extensively. These need to be handled with great sensitivity and tact by therapists, as emotions may run high and the outcome of these sessions may have long-term effects.

Family therapy for alcoholics is not simply a matter of telling the alcoholic how bad he was or presenting a litany of his faults. Rather it involves an intricate, complex discussion about how a family operates and how change is to be effected in the lives of all concerned. It is vital to talk about the problem and articulate feelings. Peace of mind is the eventual goal. Recovery for the whole family is the ideal and this is what therapists attempt to bring about. As mentioned earlier, if the alcoholic is unwilling or unable to stop drinking, it may be necessary for the rest of the family to detach themselves and make their own recovery. Full recovery also requires hard work and considerable time and patience. One estimate postulates that it takes at least eighteen months, and possibly two years, for the family system to regain normality following treatment. Recovery is always ongoing. Effective treatment may initially produce the pain of self-realisation but this relatively short-term pain should be contrasted with the long-term relief of recovery.

Unrealistic Expectations

I believe that the biggest mistake made by family members in the treatment and recovery stage is to expect that everything will be right once the alcoholic has accepted treatment and stops drinking. In practice, the first year after treatment is often fraught with difficulty. As one man said to me, 'It is like getting to know new people.' The task for the whole family is to establish a new, stable family system. The recovering alcoholic has to learn to cope with his feelings and responsibilities without recourse to alcohol. The family members can no longer blame everything on the alcoholic member. Trust is difficult to re-establish. In the early days of recovery, the alcoholic often complains of being watched too closely. This of course is entirely understandable. In addition many of the consequences of drinking may only become evident well into the early days of recovery, for example a new debt may come to the fore, or an adjustment problem with one of the children may emerge. These issues coming to light will touch on tender emotional areas for all concerned and may revive old resentments and anger. Sexual problems may abound due to tension, anxiety, fatigue and past memories. Here again, time and patience will resolve such problems when other aspects of the relationship return to normal. Referral to skilled psycho-sexual therapists may sometimes be necessary.

Given all these difficulties, it is not surprising to hear spouses in the early days of recovery sometimes saying, 'I preferred him drinking', or to hear alcoholics state, 'What more do you want? I have stopped drinking.' Everyone needs to understand that real change is required, not just in the drinking behaviour, but also in attitudes, lifestyles, social contacts and communication. Families who learn to talk openly and honestly about their feelings and who keep this up following treatment are likely to achieve the goal of recovery. All concerned need to be reassured that as the process of change takes place, things may sometimes appear to be worse before they get better (another paradox in this field). Aftercare is essential when therapists can help greatly to reassure and to explain such difficult paradoxical realities. Group therapy with fellow spouses where common difficulties are articulated is particularly beneficial at this stage.

Family members sometimes need just as much help from treatment agencies as does the alcoholic. While treatment may be initially painful in some cases, let me reiterate that this is relatively short-term and must be measured against long-term relief.

In conclusion it should be emphasised that recovery for families, although difficult to achieve, is well worth striving for. The family that recovers together is now a powerful, stable unit, with new values and attitudes that are mutually beneficial. Throughout this country there are many such families who bear witness to the benefits of family therapy.

Discussion

(a) *My husband, although not drinking, is never at home. He still goes to the pub at the same times as he used to when drinking. He is very irritable and cranky with the children. I told him to go to AA and keep reminding him to attend aftercare, but he tells me to mind my own business.*

From what you say, it does sound as if your husband is in a 'dry drunk' state; that is to say, although he is not drinking nothing much else appears to have changed. He needs help with this as he will certainly drink again if this behaviour continues. It also sounds as if your husband resents what he perceives as your trying to control his life, for example you said you told him to attend AA. I would suggest that you should back off slightly and try to take less responsibility. It is essential to achieve a balance in this area.

(b) *Why did none of us notice that my husband had become an alcoholic until he crashed his car and nearly killed himself?*

Because alcoholism is an insidious disease, its gradual development means that it can often be overlooked until some crisis, such as the one you describe, comes along.

(c) *Should I certify my husband/wife into hospital when he/she becomes violent or is in danger of harming himself/herself as my friends urge me to do? He/she has consistently refused to take treatment on a voluntary basis.*

Certification of an alcoholic is a serious step and should be employed only after careful consideration and as a last resort. Long-term resentment leading to family disruption may result. However, in extreme cases involving violence or the risk of personal harm, there may be no alternative. Your doctor will advise you.

Appendix A

Definition of Alcoholism

Alcoholism is a *primary,* chronic *disease* with genetic, psychosocial, and environmental factors influencing its development and manifestations. The disease is *often progressive and fatal.* It is characterised by continuous or periodic: *Impaired control* over drinking, *preoccupation* with the drug alcohol, use of alcohol despite *adverse consequences,* and distortions in thinking, most notably *denial.*

■ *Primary* refers to the nature of alcoholism as a disease entity in addition to and separate from other pathophysiologic states which may be associated with it. 'Primary' suggests that alcoholism, as an addiction, is not a symptom of an underlying disease state.

■ *Disease* means an involuntary disability. It represents the sum of the abnormal phenomena displayed by a group of individuals. These phenomena are associated with a specified common set of characteristics by which these individuals differ from the norm, and which places them at a disadvantage.

■ *Often progressive and fatal* means that the disease persists over time and that physical, emotional, and social changes are often cumulative and may progress as drinking continues. Alcoholism causes premature death through overdose, organic complications involving the brain, liver, heart and many other organs, and by contributing to suicide, homicide, motor vehicle crashes, and other traumatic events.

- *Impaired control* means the inability to limit alcohol use or to consistently limit on any drinking occasion the duration of the episode, the quantity consumed, and/or the behavioural consequences of drinking.

- *Preoccupation* in association with alcohol use indicates excessive, focused attention given to the drug alcohol, its effects, and/or its use. The relative value thus assigned to alcohol by the individual often leads to a diversion of energies away from important life concerns.

- *Adverse consequences* are alcohol-related problems or impairments in such areas as: physical health (e.g. alcohol withdrawal syndromes, liver disease, gastritis, anaemia, neurological disorders); psychological functioning (e.g. impairments in cognition, changes in mood and behaviour); interpersonal functioning (e.g. marital problems and child abuse, impaired social relationships); occupational functioning (e.g. scholastic or job problems); and legal, financial, or spiritual problems.

- *Denial* is used here not only in the psychoanalytic sense of a single psychological defence mechanism disavowing the significance of events, but more broadly to include a range of psychological manoeuvres designed to reduce awareness of the fact that alcohol use is the cause of an individual's problems rather than a solution to those problems. Denial becomes an integral part of the disease and a major obstacle to recovery.

Approved by the Boards of Directors of: National Council on Alcoholism and Drug Dependence (3 February 1990); American Society of Addiction Medicine (25 February 1990)

Appendix B

Questionnaires

Several questionnaires have been developed for the diagnosis of alcohol abuse. The Michigan Alcoholism Screening Test (MAST) and the 'Cage' questionnaires are regarded as particularly useful. The MAST is available in two versions: the original 25-item questionnaire which is administered by an interviewer, and a shorter self-administered version comprising the ten items of greatest discriminatory value. A score of five points or more on the brief MAST is taken as diagnostic of alcohol abuse.

Brief MAST

Circle correct answer

Do you feel you are a normal drinker? ....YES   NO(2pts)

Do friends or relatives think you
are a normal drinker? ....YES   NO(2pts)

Have you ever attended a meeting of
Alcoholics Anonymous? ....YES(5pts) NO

Have you ever lost friends or girlfriends
or boyfriends because of drinking? ....YES(2 pts) NO

Have you ever got into trouble at
work because of drinking? ....YES(2pts) NO

Have you ever neglected your obligations,
your family, or your work for two or more
days in a row because you were drinking? ...YES(2pts) NO

Have you ever had delirium tremens (DTs),
severe shaking, heard voices or seen things
that were not there after heavy drinking? ...YES(5pts) NO

Have you ever gone to anyone
for help about your drinking? ....YES(5pts)   NO
Have you ever been in a hospital
because of drinking? ....YES(5pts)   NO
Have you ever been arrested for
drunken driving or driving
after drinking? ....YES(2pts)   NO

Total score ....

(From Pokorny A.D., Miller B.A., Kaplan H.B., *American Journal of Psychiatry* 1972; 129: 342–5)

Cage

In some cases the Cage questionnaire is more appropriate. Two or more positive replies are said to identify problem drinkers.

Have you ever felt you ought to *cut* down on your drinking?
Have people *annoyed* you by criticising your drinking?
Have you ever felt bad or *guilty* about your drinking?
Have you ever had a drink first thing in the morning to steady your nerves or get rid of a hangover? ('eye opener')

(From Mayfield D., McLeod G., Hall P. *American Journal of Psychiatry* 1974; 131: 1121–3)

It must be emphasised that the questionnaires are not 100% accurate. While they may act as pointers to the possible existence of an alcohol problem, they depend on honest replies which may not always be forthcoming. They must never be regarded as adequate substitutes for a properly conducted interview. For example, patients with physical diseases caused by alcohol may never have suffered any of the social consequences of heavy drinking. Indeed their drinking habits may have been regarded as socially quite acceptable so that such patients would be missed by this type of questionnaire.

Appendix C

Treatment

This term is widely used but seldom defined. It may cover a range of approaches from minimal intervention to comprehensive management of alcohol dependence.

In 1980 the American Medical Society on Alcoholism (AMSA) adopted the statement on the treatment of alcoholism set out below.

By 1986 AMSA had broadened its activities to include other drug dependencies and changed its title to the American Medical Society on Alcoholism and Other Drug Dependence (AMSOD). In line with this change, it modified the 1980 statement to include the treatment of drug dependencies other than alcohol.

Statement on treatment for alcoholism

I. GENERAL DEFINITION OF TREATMENT
Treatment for alcoholism is the use of any planned, intentional intervention in the health, behaviour, personal and/or family life of an individual suffering from alcoholism, designed to enable the affected individual to achieve and maintain sobriety, physical and mental health, and maximum functional ability.

II. COMPONENTS OF TREATMENT
Treatment of alcoholism should include all or a combination of the following:
1. A thorough physical and psychosocial evaluation.
2. Detoxification: that is, the achievement of a state free of both alcohol and sedative drugs. Detoxification may be

accomplished on an in-patient or out-patient basis, and with or without the use of psychoactive drugs, depending on the physical, psychological and social needs of the patient.

3. Counselling, including education on: the nature of alcoholism as a disease; the need for long-term abstinence; the need for a programme of rehabilitation, including family involvement; the dangers of addiction to other drugs, and other related issues.

4. Medical treatment of the physical concomitants and complications of alcoholism, including attention to nutritional needs.

5. Psychological assistance for the patient and family through psychotherapy and/or counselling, along with involvement in self-help groups, depending on the needs and characteristics of the patient and the family. This assistance is aimed at sustaining motivation for sobriety, and helping the patient find alternative healthier ways of coping with personal, work, family and social problems without dependence on alcohol. It is aimed at helping the family develop healthier, more satisfying patterns of interaction which will in turn facilitate and reinforce the patient's sobriety. This includes help for the children of patients with alcoholism aimed also at prevention of the disease in this high-risk group.

   The prescription of a deterrent drug such as Disulfiram,* or aversive counter-conditioning may accompany this phase of treatment as a motivational aid.

6. Treatment of any psychiatric illness which may accompany the alcoholism, such as severe depression, neurotic or psychotic conditions, or sexual disorders.

7. Referral for help with social, legal, child care, vocational, spiritual or other associated problems to appropriate community resources.

8. Long term follow-up. Since alcoholism is a chronic disease, treatment is generally conducted as a planned programme with a prolonged follow-up, or on an open-ended basis.

III. LENGTH OF TREATMENT

Depending on the age of the patient, the stage of illness, the degree of associated physical and psychiatric disability,

and the extent of social, family, vocational and legal problems, the length of the treatment and rehabilitation process
will vary widely from case to case. In all cases, however, long-
term availability of social supports and medical supervision
are needed because of the chronic nature of the illness and
potential for relapse.

IV. TREATMENT SETTINGS
Depending on the same combination of factors cited under
Length of Treatment, the process of treatment may take place
in one of a variety of settings or a combination of settings:

1. In-patient
   a. general hospital with alcoholism programme
   b. free-standing alcoholism facility
   c. free-standing alcoholism and drug unit combined
   d. general hospital alcoholism and drug unit combined
   e. psychiatric hospital, community mental health centre

2. Other residential
   a. alcoholism recovery home
   b. 'social model' detoxification
   c. halfway house, or hostel
   d. sobering-up station
   e. 'night hospital'

3. Out-patient
   a. clinic
   b. day programme
   c. drop-in centre
   d. emergency/crisis intervention
   e. information and referral agency
   f. office of private practitioner

V. TREATMENT PROVIDERS
Treatment for alcoholism is often the result of a co-operative
effort between a number of professional and non-professional
persons, most frequently including

1. Medical
   a. physician, including internists, family physicians,
      psychiatrists, paediatricians, and others
   b. physician assistant

2. Nursing
   a. nurse
   b. nurse practitioner

3. Other professionals
   a. alcoholism counsellor
   b. psychologist
   c. social worker
   d. vocational rehabilitation counsellor
   e. nutritionist/dietician
   f. health educator
   g. member of clergy

4. Non-professionals
   a. voluntary members of self-help groups
   b. volunteers involved in information and referral services

VI. SELF-HELP GROUPS

Self-help groups for persons suffering from alcoholism and for their families have been and remain a vital source of help in recovery. They represent a long-term and ongoing source of psychological, social and spiritual intervention and support, and are recommended as part of the plan of treatment wherever possible.

(Adopted by the American Medical Society on Alcoholism (AMSA), 4 May 1980)

* Dulsifiram is marketed as Antabuse (see Chapter 6).

Appendix D

Alcoholics Anonymous, Al-Anon, Alateen

ALCOHOLICS ANONYMOUS

Alcoholics Anonymous is a fellowship of men and women who share their experience, strength and hope with each other that they may solve their common problem and help others to recover from alcoholism.

* The only requirement for membership is a desire to stop drinking. There are no dues or fees for AA membership; we are self-supporting through our own contributions.

* AA is not allied with any sect, denomination, politics, organisation or institution; does not wish to engage in any controversy; neither endorses nor opposes any causes.

* Our primary purpose is to stay sober and help other alcoholics to achieve sobriety.

This statement which is read at the beginning of every AA meeting sets out the position of Alcoholics Anonymous.

The movement was born in Akron, Ohio, USA in 1935 when a local physician, Bob, suffering from alcohol addiction, met a New York stockbroker, Bill, himself a victim of the disease. By a happy chance, Bill had come to terms with his alcoholism some months earlier due to his acceptance of some of the tenets of the Oxford Movement, as well as the assistance he had received from Dr William D. Silkworth, a New York specialist in alcoholism. Bob was so impressed by Bill's recovery that he determined to follow his lead and by so doing succeeded in attaining sobriety which he maintained up to his death in 1950. Together, Bob and Bill set to work on alcoholics admitted to the Akron City Hospital and straightaway brought an advanced case of alcoholism to recovery. Success was subsequently achieved with some other alcoholics. By the end of 1935 the first AA group had in effect been formed.

The movement then spread to New York. By 1939 it had grown to the stage where it had attracted many new members and in this same year published the first edition of the book *Alcoholics Anonymous*, popularly known as 'The Big Book'. This publication became its basic text. During the 1930s, much attention was given to formulating a philosophy for the movement. This eventually became enshrined in 'The Twelve Steps of Alcoholics Anonymous'.

1. We admitted we were powerless over alcohol — that our lives had become unmanageable.
2. Came to believe that a Power greater than ourselves could restore us to sanity.
3. Made a decision to turn our will and our lives over to the care of God *as we understood Him.*
4. Made a searching and fearless moral inventory of ourselves.
5. Admitted to God, to ourselves and to another human being the exact nature of our wrongs.
6. Were entirely ready to have God remove all these defects of character.
7. Humbly asked Him to remove our shortcomings.
8. Made a list of all persons we had harmed, and became willing to make amends to them all.
9. Made direct amends to such people wherever possible, except when to do so would injure them or others.
10. Continued to take personal inventory and when we were wrong promptly admitted it.
11. Sought through prayer and meditation to improve our conscious contact with God, *as we understood Him,* praying only for knowledge of His will for us and the power to carry that out.
12. Having had a spiritual awakening as the result of these steps, we tried to carry this message to alcoholics, and to practise these principles in all our affairs.

From its modest beginnings AA spread rapidly, with a spectacular acceleration of growth in the post-war years. Today it is widely established throughout the whole world and is the largest self-help group in existence. Since its foundation it has enabled countless victims of alcoholism, embracing both sexes, all ages, classes and many races to arrest the disease on the basis of sobriety. Essentially its conversion is achieved by the application of the maxim that the alcoholic should concentrate on his sobriety one day at a time, i.e. the 24 hour plan. Its operation is governed by 'The Twelve Traditions of Alcoholics Anonymous'.

1. Our common welfare should come first; personal recovery depends upon AA unity.
2. For our group purpose there is but one ultimate authority — a loving God as He may express Himself in our group conscience. Our leaders are but trusted servants; they do not govern.
3. The only requirement for AA membership is a desire to stop drinking.
4. Each group should be autonomous except in matters affecting other groups or AA as a whole.
5. Each group has but one primary purpose — to carry its message to the alcoholic who still suffers.
6. An AA group ought never endorse, finance, or lend the AA name to any related facility or outside enterprise, lest problems of money, property, and prestige divert us from our primary purpose.
7. Every AA group ought to be fully self-supporting, declining outside contributions.
8. Alcoholics Anonymous should remain forever non-professional, but our service centres may employ special workers.
9. AA, as such, ought never be organised; but we may create service boards or committees directly responsible to those they serve.
10. Alcoholics Anonymous has no opinion on outside issues; hence the AA name ought never be drawn into public controversy.

11. Our public relations policy is based on attraction rather than promotion; we need always maintain personal anonymity at the level of press, radio, and films.
12. Anonymity is the spiritual foundation of all our traditions, ever reminding us to place principles before personalities.

Over the years I have been greatly impressed, not just by the real sense of fellowship which obtains between AA members, but by their selflessness. At all times they are only too willing to inconvenience themselves to whatever degree may be necessary in order to help other victims of alcoholism. In common with those of my medical colleagues who, like myself, are engaged in the treatment of alcohol abuse and alcoholism, I have good reason to be grateful to the members of AA and their associated organisations, Al-Anon and Alateen, for their ready assistance with my work over the years. This co-operation is in accordance with the tradition of AA going back to its origins in the 1930s when Dr Silkworth featured so prominently.

In Ireland we have been fortunate to have an active AA movement in place since 1946, thanks to the single-mindedness of Conor F., an Irish immigrant to Philadelphia, who returned on a visit to his native land determined to bring to Ireland the AA message which had been responsible for his own recovery from alcoholism some years earlier. I am deeply grateful to him for the following account of his 'odyssey'.

> One evening while in Co. Derry and watching the rain pelting down, my wife showed me an article in the *Evening Mail* (a Dublin paper). A four line article given by a Fr Dunlee who, like myself, was another immigrant home on a holiday. Fr Dunlee ran a Boys Town in Australia, and while giving an interview to a reporter from the *Evening Mail*, a Mr Mair, Fr Dunlee mentioned briefly that he felt there was a need for Alcoholics Anonymous in Dublin. Very few, if any, ever heard of Alcoholics Anonymous in Ireland, also, a lot of people in the States never heard of the Fellowship of AA.

I set out for Dublin with my little bit of literature and the few big books. I told myself that if there was any place in Ireland for me to start an AA group it would have to be in Dublin. That was the first of my many mistakes and I found that out as I went along. There were some who thought I might have a 'screw loose' and I was just a lucky immigrant home on a holiday. In Dublin I was lucky to get an interview with Mr Mair of the *Evening Mail*. The article I gave him I thought was very good and it was front page publicity. I thought I had it made. I added a box number to the article and got 26 replies. A few smart alecks who wanted something for their signature. I was sure with this front page publicity the phone would never stop ringing. I was disappointed. I showed my article to many people; they just looked at it and smiled and said, 'A new fangled article like you have should be great for America but not very good for Ireland, the people in Ireland don't drink very much and if there were an odd one here and there the Pioneer movement can take care of them.' Some asked me why I thought the Irish were hard drinkers.

I was having breakfast with a social worker by the name of Eva. I told Eva I was leaving Dublin and going to Co. Derry. Eva said, 'I saw you come in last night and I thought you had a few jars on you.' I said no Eva but I could have used one. At last I had confided to another person what I was trying to do. I told Eva that I was coming from one of the large institutions the night before. And I was told they never had alcoholics in the institution. Eva said, 'Did they tell you that Conor?' I said they surely did. Eva said, 'I have a surprise for you Conor. My brother is in that hospital for the past week getting dried out.' I told her I was about to give up. I said the alcoholics in Dublin are not the same as we have in Philadelphia, and Eva said, 'Alcoholics are the same all over the world.' Then I decided to make one more call and, like Eva instructed me, 'Talk to Norman

Moore, head of St Patrick's Hospital.' I was sure I would get the bum's rush, but no, I got a very nice reception from Dr Moore who was very patient with me. I left him a 'Big Book' and some literature. He told me he had given the 'Big Book' to one of his patients who was down in Lucan, and if I wanted to meet this man he would bring him to St Patrick's the next day. I felt great; someone at last thought I had something to offer and it was Dr Moore the first man in the medical profession in the British Isles to endorse the Fellowship of AA. I met Richard, hand-picked by Dr Moore; he was my right-hand. Only God knows how many people came through St Patrick's on their way to AA. Dr Moore sent Richard to AA, the first man in the British Isles to stand up before an open meeting and state that he had a drinking problem and he had joined the fellowship of AA. We shall always be grateful to Dr Moore for his great contribution to AA and to many of its members. We have had many nice days in Ireland. Possibly Eva is right. Alcoholics are the same all over the world.

Signed: Conor F.

From this small beginning the AA movement spread to the UK and then to the continent of Europe. This development, and the fact that approximately 550 branches of AA are in existence throughout the country, highlights the success of Conor F.'s initiative.

AL-ANON

The Al-Anon movement is concerned with the spouses of alcoholics. It too employs the group principle and has achieved widespread success. Its members meet regularly, discuss their feelings and reactions to the abnormal drinking of their family members and learn to cope with the situation. The organisation makes use of 'The Twelve Steps of AA' and has adopted the guidelines of the 'The Twelve Traditions of AA' as the basis of its operation. The Al-Anon movement has been highly successful in its aims as has Alateen.

138

ALATEEN

This is an organisation operating on similar lines to Al-Anon. It caters for the teenage children of alcoholics.

SERENITY PRAYER

While this is used commonly in all three organisations, to my mind its sentiments have a universal appeal and would bring comfort to all persons troubled in mind or spirit.

> God, grant us the serenity to accept the
> things we cannot change,
> Courage to change the things we can,
> And wisdom to know the difference.

Appendix E

Help and Advice

To find out where to get help, advice and assistance, contact:

1. Your general practitioner.
2. Your local health board.
3. The Health Promotion Unit,
    Department of Health
    Hawkins House
    Dublin 2 (Tel. 01–714711)
4. Alcoholics Anonymous
    General Service Office
    109 South Circular Road
    Dublin 8 (Tel. 01–538998)
5. Al-Anon Information Office
    1st Floor
    5 Capel Street
    Dublin 1 (Tel. 01–732699)
6. Adult Children of Alcoholics (ACOA)
    St Patrick's Hospital
    James Street
    Dublin 8 (Tel. 01–775423)

Index

144